W9-BHL-955

# GULLAH GEECHEE
## HOME COOKING

# GULLAH GEECHEE
## HOME COOKING

RECIPES *from the* MATRIARCH *of* EDISTO ISLAND

**EMILY MEGGETT**

**with Kayla Stewart and Trelani Michelle**

Photography by Clay Williams

ABRAMS, NEW YORK

# TABLE *of* CONTENTS

*"You were always bound to get something good to eat. I thought she was God, could make anything. I wanted to be just like her."*

—DENISE RANDALL-RAVANEL, MY OLDEST GRANDCHILD

# WELCOME *to* EDISTO ISLAND

WHEN YOU CROSS THE DAWHOO BRIDGE THAT CONNECTS EDISTO ISLAND TO THE REST OF SOUTH CAROLINA, YOU'RE IN HEAVEN. HEAVEN ON EARTH, THAT IS.

I'm Emily Hutchinson Meggett. Most people know me as "M.P." I was born on Edisto Island, South Carolina, on November 19, 1932.

Forty-two miles south of Charleston and home to just over 2,000 people, Edisto Island was a place where everyone knew everyone when I was growing up. There wasn't much out on the island then. The one way on, one way off Dawhoo Bridge was just a plank bridge. Highway 174 used to be just a dirt road. Some of the landmarks I remember on Highway 174 are the Eubank Store, Seaside Elementary, Edisto Post Office, Zion Church, Trinity Episcopal Church, New First Baptist Church, and Larimer High School.

Though small, this island is one of the most blessed places on earth. Edisto has these great, big live oak trees that are full of Spanish moss, so many different types of animals—birds and fish especially—and a beach that has some of the biggest shells you've ever seen in your life. On this island, we're insulated versus isolated (to quote Queen Quet, the Chieftess of the Gullah Geechee nation) from the hustle and bustle of city life. So Edisto maintains a sense of peace and stillness that my people have lived with for many generations.

Many of my ancestors and elders would work in fields during the day, growing cotton, corn, potatoes, and other vegetables, then go home and tend to their own gardens. My grandparents owned ten acres of land. We didn't have no fertilizer for the garden. Mama would use manure from the chicken house, the horse stable, and the cow pen. We had corn (white and yellow), butter beans, lima beans, peas, black-eyed and field peas, okra, watermelon, cantaloupe, squash, onions, tomatoes, sweet potatoes, white potatoes, sugarcane, sugar millet, and our own rice pond. We had chicken, turkey, duck; we had fowl, hogs; we had horses.

We didn't have to go to the store for any fresh vegetables, either. We just went for items like sugar and flour. That's because, like generations before us, we grew our own vegetables and there were plenty of fruit trees. We were so blessed. We even had our own livestock for meat, and my uncles would bring back plenty from fishing and hunting. Raccoon, squirrel, and quail—we ate all of that. I remember them hanging the coon from a tree and skinning it. When they got through skinning it, they'd salt it then leave it for a day or two to dry—sometimes outside in the tree, other times on ice. Let it dry out and then take it down and cut it up, soak it for an hour or two, and cook it. If it's cooked the right way, you can't tell if it's chicken or turkey. Now that's some good cooking, I'll tell ya.

When my grandmother and uncle and those would kill cows and pigs, they had a little smokehouse outside. Whatever they was gon' smoke, they smoked it. Whatever they wasn't gon' smoke, they preserved it in the ground. The guy would come around and bring the ice. They'd dig a hole in the ground, put the ice in the ground in a brown bag along with whatever meat they got. They'd wrap it up, lay it on that ice, put a piece of rooftop tin on that ice to keep the dirt out, and cover it up. And the ice would last for days. They

*LEFT TO RIGHT: A welcome sign to Edisto Island; crabs from South Carolina; an Edisto marsh; Indigo Hill, home of the matriarch; the Hutchinson House on Edisto Island*

didn't have no refrigerator. We didn't get a refrigerator until the early fifties.

Because we had our own rice pond, we harvested our own rice. Rice is a big deal to the Gullah Geechee people. Most of us have roots in Sierra Leone, a country known for its legacy of skilled rice farmers who could grow and cook rice. Just as it is with us, rice is served with most dishes there, too. We also harvested our own sugarcane, and when the corn was ready to be picked, whether it was yellow or white corn, we'd have it ground into grits. My uncle 'Nem would break the corn and put it in the back of the horse and buggy. On Wednesday, we'd shuck the corn. On Thursday and Friday, we'd have to shell the corn off the cob and put it in these big ol' bags. Then, on Saturday, a man would come from Jericho, which was about twenty miles out, and pick up the corn and take it to Jericho Mill. When they got through processing the corn, they would bring it back, and you would have a twenty-five- or fifty-pound bag of grits and another of husks. The same with the white one and the yellow one. Then you'd have the cornmeal, the yellow and the white. That's what you ate off of for the winter, so you didn't have to go to the store. The husks went to the hogs.

See, as most cities moved toward becoming more industrial, Edisto was still agricultural. We held on to the old ways of doing things for a very long time, some of it still to this day. Working the land is one of them. It was our way of surviving. It's how we fed ourselves, empowered ourselves, and kept our ancestral ties intact.

My family tree is deeply rooted in Edisto. In fact, my great-grandfather, Jim Hutchinson, was known as one of the "Kings of Edisto Island." He was born in 1836 on Peters Point Plantation. According to our family history, his mother, Maria, was enslaved to his father, Isaac Jenkins Mikell, the plantation owner. He served the country during the Civil War, then got involved in local politics. A letter my great-grandfather wrote to the governor at the time, Robert Scott, resulted in a good bit of plantation land being divided among freed black people. One of his sons, Henry (my grandfather's brother), built a family home around 1885 that still stands today: the Hutchinson House.

Like many Black people in the thirties and forties, my mother, Laura Hutchinson, joined the Great Migration and moved north to earn more money. So my grandmother Elizabeth Major Hutchinson and my uncles, Isaiah and Luther Hutchinson, raised me. One of my uncles lived in the house with us. My other uncle lived in Charleston. When everybody saw his light-blue pickup truck bumping down the road, you'd think Santa Claus was coming. He'd be passing out apples, oranges, candy, and shoes. Sometimes he'd even bring furniture that folk from the city had thrown out.

When I say "mama," I'm referring to my grandmother. Mama, my uncle, his wife, me, my sister Bernice, and my cousins Marion, Edmond, Sonny, James, Emma, Jesse, and Gillie all lived under the same roof at the same time. We ate together, too. Whoever didn't fit at the kitchen table ate at the dining room table. We ate our meals as a family, though, and when I became a mother, I did my best to keep that tradition going.

Back then, we didn't have no radio or TV. We made our own fun by yanking the vine out of the tree to jump rope, pulling roots out the ground for a doll baby, putting a rope in the tree for a swing, and making our own hopscotch. Growing up, I went to several schools on Edisto Island: Seaside Elementary School, Central School, and Larimer High School. Mama would wake us up at five o'clock in the morning, including on school days, to do our chores. We had to go in the field, hoe two rows of okra, two rows of beans and corn, then come home, wash up, and eat breakfast. We never left the house without our breakfast of butt's meat (also known as salt pork) and wild cat sauce on grits, and biscuits.

We'd have to be at school by eight o'clock and walk five miles to get there, but we'd make such a good time out of it that it didn't feel like it was that long. Sometimes we had so much fun, we'd mess around and be late. The teacher told us one day, "If y'all are late tomorrow, everybody is gonna get punished with twenty-four chops—twelve in the left hand and twelve in the right." Corporal punishment was legal in schools at that time.

Well, we were late that next day. To avoid the hand chops, we went to a place called Long Reach instead of going to school. When we walked through Long Reach, we could see some of our grandmothers, mine included, working in the fields. Since they weren't home, we went to their house and cooked fry bread with sugar. Fry bread and pancake are the same, just given a different name. Same ingredients. I grew up with fry bread. Waffle is the same mixture, but it's just a different texture. With pancake or fry bread, you mix the sugar, egg, and Crisco together.

There were after-school chores too. You take your school clothes off, get in your old clothes, then go in the field and pump the water for the cow, feed the hog, feed the chickens, tie the cow on fresh grass, fasten the chickens up, gather the eggs, bring in the wood, pump the water to bring in the house. Everybody had a job, and everybody knew how to do everything. In the wintertime, boys would cut the wood and the girls would bring it in. We would also go out in the field and gather straw to make the broom to sweep the floor with, and wood for the fireplace. There was no mop to mop the floor. You would scrub the floor on your knees with water in a bucket, and a rag and the octagon powder. After scrubbing the floor, it would come out so clean you could eat off it. There were no rakes to rake the yard; we'd take the branches off the trees and use them to rake the yard. It would come just as clean as if you had a rake, it was amazing.

Life was very different in those days. There was no washing machine or dryer. We didn't have Clorox. You'd put your clothes in this big boiler and you boil it, and they would come out as white as a piece of paper. There was no bathroom, you had to go to an outside toilet. No electric stove; we had a woodstove, a kerosene lamp, and a lantern. No screen in the window, so, hot or cold, the mosquitoes always had a good time. We'd make smoke in a pot with rags, moss, or trash, and that would run the mosquitoes away. Back then lots of people didn't have a clock; the time was in their heads. They would say when the sun gets in the middle of the door, it was twelve o'clock, lunchtime, and it's true.

We were poor, by most standards. Making something out of nothing was our specialty. And recycling and repurposing was all we knew. Mama didn't throw away anything, and to this day, I don't believe in wasting anything, so I don't throw nothin' away too. Everything Mama had, she made something good for it. Whether it was food or clothes, she'd take the littlest thing and turn it into gold. We might've had to work harder for it, but our food was always fresh. Like how we churned our own butter. It would smell so good, rich as I don't know what! It didn't even need to be kept cold; we'd just store it on the shelf.

Growing food, raising livestock, and knowing how to preserve were traditions passed down from our ancestors way back in Africa. They brought those skills here with them and we continued them. What makes us Gullah Geechee is just a matter of time and

*LEFT TO RIGHT: Emily's daughter Mildred Meggett Heyward; New First Missionary Baptist Church ushers Z'Niyah Holmes, Rayanna Fludd, LaShonda Burnell, Jalashia Black, Darryl Hill, Shamar Snipes, Shatabia Simmons, Igah Hill, DeeKee Lang, Amarion Taylor, Jayla Hill, and Kamille Horn; my daughter Carolyn Meggett; Emily's son Christopher Hutchinson; Mildred Megget Heyward and Emily Meggett; Emily's uncle Cornelius Thrower and mother, Laura V. Hutchinson*

place. Our ancestors were brought from West Africa to the coast of South Carolina, Georgia, and Florida. What makes the Gullah Geechee people particularly special is how long we've been able to hold on to our old ways, including the way we speak and the way we eat.

Mama always kept food on the stove. She would always say, "Don't ever cook enough just for you, 'cause you never know who gonna come through that door." I got my love for cooking from my grandmother. My generosity, too. When I was growing up, our house was like the community center. All the neighborhood children would come by to eat. Though we didn't have much, there was always enough to share. Mama made sure she taught us the importance of taking care of people too, and I've been doing it since I was a small child. She would cook and have me take it to the elderly people in that community. That stuck with me.

Other things have stuck with me, too. Throughout this book, you'll see stories that I've shared with close friends and family, stories about my life, and the lives of those around me. Some are observations; some are recollections of important life events.

I spent most of my childhood in the same house, and that house was destroyed in a storm in 1940. I was seven years old, but I remember it vividly. I later learned that it was a category 2 hurricane that killed thirty-four people and destroyed plenty of property along the Georgia–South Carolina coast. They didn't evacuate us back in those times, so we were home when the storm hit. Mama would cook lima beans, crowder peas, collard greens, something that would feed a whole lot of people whenever a storm

was coming. Storms on the island are much different from those on the mainland. I remember sitting on the porch, splashing my feet in the rising water while my cousin whined to our grandmother that we were hungry. She would say, "I'm preparing food for when the storm come. When it come and you can't cook, what you gonna do? We gonna save that food for that hard time." We'd be thinking, *It's hard time now!*



We didn't have much money, but we were still rich. We were full of love and wisdom. I carried those values into my adult life. I got married to Jessie Meggett, who was also born on the island, in 1932. We had a small yard wedding, but our marriage lasted fifty-five and a half years. I kept my promise, 'til death did us part. My dress cost $19.99 and Jessie's suit was $39. After the ceremony, my uncle took us on our honeymoon in the back of the pickup truck. Jessie and I was in the truck and he drove us to the turntable on Edisto Beach, then we just turned around and came back home. For the reception, Mama made us homemade cherry wine and pound cake. When we had our real honeymoon it was in 1980; we went to Germany, Paris, London, then come home. That was the best honeymoon anyone could ever have, thirty-one years later.

We had ten children together, Christopher, Mildred, Elizann, Joann, Louise, Emily, Carolyn, Lavern, Elizabeth, and Marvette, and one stepson, Ronald. We lived modest and within our means, never in a rush, so our family never went without. In 1960, for instance, we purchased one acre of land for $75. In 1962, we started building a four-room house. To build that house, it costs us $1,025. In those four rooms, there were twelve of us: ten children and husband and wife. Four girls in one bed and four girls in

***"Marriage is a daily thing. Just 'cause you worked at it yesterday, doesn't mean you get by today. You work at it today, tomorrow, and every day."***

the next bed. Chris slept on the folding cot in the kitchen, and the baby slept with us in the bed. In 1969, we added more rooms to make a thirteen-room house, and we never had a mortgage.

I have taken care of more than a hundred children, besides my own—some of whom were raised in my home, with my children. Throughout the years, I have fed too many people to count. Wherever I go, it is important to me that I do not go empty-handed. I always bring a gift of food.

Cooking brings me great joy. As a teenager, I worked as a babysitter, helping to care for the children of "the help," and white people's children, too. One day, Mama told me I needed to decide: I could work in the field, or somewhere else. Now, I like my garden and I like being outside, but I don't like no field. I chose to work in the kitchen, and that decision changed my life. I have cooked in houses all over Edisto, beginning in 1954. I learned these recipes from my grandmother and Ms. Julia W. Brown, a Gullah woman from Edisto (Cedar Hall), and one of the best cooks on the island. I met Ms. Brown when I first started cooking for the Dodges, a white family from Rockport, Maine, in the oil business. We called their home, our workplace, the Dodge House. I cooked for the Dodge House for forty-five winters. Ms. Julia Brown, the head of the kitchen, told me, "You do it right or you do it over." That's how I learned to cook.

***"Don't ever cook enough just for you, 'cause you never know who gonna come through that door."***

For me, cooking wasn't just a job, it was my life, and it still is today. Cooking is how I take care of people, how I support my community, and how I love others the way God intended. When I cook, I don't just cook for me or my family—oh, no. I cook for my neighbor, for the family friends on the beach, for the plumber who stops by to fix my appliances. I believe that food is one of the most important ways we take care of each other, and I'll tell ya, nobody leaves my house without a to-go plate.

As a Black American woman, I know that I'm not the only one who has taken care of people through food, and I'm not the only one who's worked as a professional cook. Ms. Julia Brown was a head chef at the Dodge House, yet she didn't have that title, nor did they pay her what a white cook with similar experience would've been paid. Many Black women—including those whose names have been lost to history—paved the way for cooks like me to find a career that could support my family and give me the chance to do something I'm good at. Abby Fisher, Zephyr Wright, and Edna Lewis are

***RIGHT:** Jessie Meggett, my late husband*

some of the women whose contributions have changed the face of American cooking, and I'm grateful that we not only know their names, but know of the tastes, love, and joy they shared with others through food.

My life's work has taken me to many places I never realized I'd go. I've talked to journalists at national newspapers, I've cooked for large church functions, and I've mentored some of the most important young Gullah Geechee chefs of today's generation who will carry on our culture's legacy into new generations. Shoot, they even have video of me cooking my famous stuffed fish (page 71); people all over the world have watched this video and have learned just a bit about this beautiful place, and the beautiful culture behind it. Cooking teaches, cooking heals, and cooking loves.

I am so grateful for the life I've built around food and cooking in my beloved home. Now, it's important for me to share these recipes. To me, sharing home cooking is what truly represents Gullah Geechee food. I want future generations to understand the cooking and the culture of this place, and to understand that cooking is much more than about how something tastes—it's about the heart and soul behind the stove. My present and my past is in every single plate of food I cook, and I hope it's in yours, too. Knowing our history gives us a chance to look back and see where we came from. And now I share this knowledge with you. Remember what I told you now: When you cross that bridge, you're in heaven.

Welcome to my home, my heaven, and my life through food. I hope and pray this book will bring you joy, inspiration, and some good eatin'. Bring your appetite, it's time to eat.

God bless.

***"People on Edisto know if that side door is open, there is food in this kitchen. At this house there are no guests—just friends and family."***

Coosawhatchie
Pocotaligo
CHARLESTON & SAVANNAH R. R.
Gopher Hill
Grahamville
Ferebeeville
Purysburg
Hardeeville
Coosawhatchie R.
Tullifiny River
Pocotaligo River
Hall I.
Garden's Corner
Combahee
Barnwell I.
Long Pt.
Whale Branch
Port Royal Ferry
Whale I.
Keans Neck
S O U T H
LEMON ISD.
Broad River
PORT ROYAL ISD.
Chisholm
Middleton Swamp
BEAUFORT
Battery Cr.
Fort
LADIES ISLAND
Coosaw River
Bull River
Bluffton
Buck Pt.
Colleton River
Colleton Neck
Chechessee River
DAW I.
Archer's Cr.
Horse I.
Coosaw I.
Morgan I.
PARRY I.
Beaufort River
Cane I.
Wassaw I.
Dathaw I.
Morgan River
May River
Savage I.
Page I.
Pine I.
HULL ISLAND
Barntarts I.
PINKNEY I.
Cooper River
DAUFUSKIE ISLAND
Marsh I.
CALIBOGUE SOUND
HILTON HEAD ISLAND
Ft. Walker
Hilton Head
Braddock's Pt.
PORT ROYAL ENTRANCE
ST. HELENA ISLAND
Lands End
Flats
PHILLIPS' I.
Ft. Beauregard
Egg Bank
Harbor R.
Harbor I.
Trenchard's Inlet
St. Michael's Pt.
Capers I.
Pritchard's I.
Fripp's I.
Hunting I.
Pritchard's Inlet
Skull Inlet
Fripps Inlet
Statute Miles
1 ½ 0 5 10 15 20
Scale 1: 200.000.

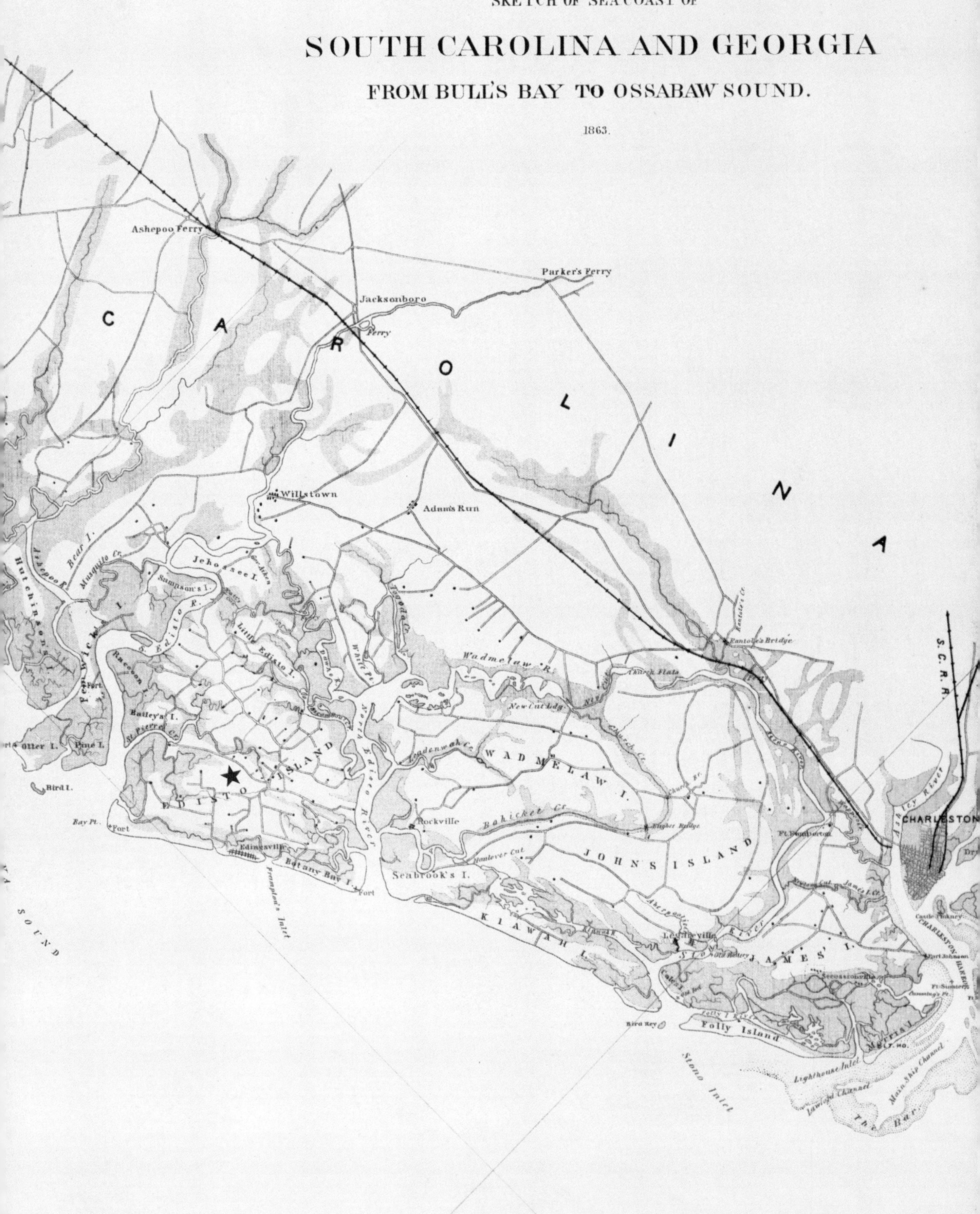
SKETCH OF SEA COAST OF
SOUTH CAROLINA AND GEORGIA
FROM BULL'S BAY TO OSSABAW SOUND.
1863.
CAROLINA
Ashepoo Ferry
Parker's Ferry
Jacksonboro
Ferry
Willstown
Adams Run
Rantole's Bridge
S. C. R. R.
Wadmelaw R.
New Cut Ldg.
Church Flats
Church Cr.
Ashepoo R.
Hutchinson's I.
Bear I.
Musquito Cr.
Jehossee I.
Sampson's I.
S. Edisto R.
Little Edisto I.
Fenwick's I.
Raccoon I.
Bailey's I.
Otter I.
Pine I.
Bird I.
Bay Pt.
Fort
EDISTO ISLAND
Edingsville
Botany Bay I.
North Edisto River
WADMELAW I.
Bohicket Cr.
Rockville
Seabrook's I.
Haulover Cut
JOHNS ISLAND
Ft. Pemberton
Ashley River
CHARLESTON
KIAWAH I.
Legareville
JAMES' I.
Secessionville
Castle Pinkney
Fort Johnson
CHARLESTON HARBOR
Ft. Sumter
Folly Island
Bird Key
Stono Inlet
Lighthouse Inlet
Lawford Channel
Main Ship Channel
The Bar
SOUND

# *The* AMERICAN STORY *of the* GULLAH GEECHEE PEOPLE

WHEN I WAS GROWING UP, I ALWAYS THOUGHT I WAS JUST BLACK. I KNEW I WAS BLACK. I could see Black in my parents; I could hear Black from the people who lived near me; I could taste Black in the kitchen. But then I went to school, and somebody told me that I was Geechee.

*Geechee?* I say to myself. *What's Geechee?* For all I knew, I was just Black. I was a Black woman who was born and raised on a beautiful Sea Island called Edisto Island. My parents were Black, my family was Black, my community was Black. What was all of this Geechee that people were talking about?

As I got older, come to find out, my culture and history were Black, yes, but there was more to the story. I realized that I was a descendant of the Gullah Geechee people, a group of enslaved Africans who managed to maintain culture, tradition, and identity despite centuries of enslavement and enduring racism in the American South.

Now, here's the thing about being what I now call "Gullah" or "Geechee." (You can use the terms interchangeably, which you will see I do in this book.) I didn't grow up being told that this was Gullah or Geechee, that was Gullah or Geechee—no. The culture was simply part of my life. It was in the red rice we'd often eat with fried fish for dinner during the week; it was in the language and dialect I used to communicate with other Gullah people on the island; and most important, it was in my history.

Through this lineage, I know that my family, like many of Gullah descent, had incredible agricultural and rice cultivation knowledge. The legacy of rice farming runs deep in my family, extending all the way through my own grandparents, and reflects what we know about Gullah Geechee people: Our community began with African enslaved people who had advanced knowledge of farming, and unique relationships with the land and sea.

The history of the Gullah people begins in Africa. These people were captured from their homeland and forcibly migrated to the southern coasts of the United States as early as the 1500s. South Carolina received a large portion of these enslaved people. Records from the Port of Charleston show that enslaved Africans arrived from countries and regions like Angola, Senegambia, Sierra Leone, the Gold Coast, and Benin. When they arrived, they were greeted by land that was very similar to their former homes: The temperatures were hot and humid, the water was grayish blue and crisp, and the land was fertile and ready for farming.

The cruelty in this was that, in spite of the physical similarities, this new land would be nothing like the African nations these enslaved people used to call home. These Africans were immediately thrown into backbreaking labor, families were split apart because of white American greed, and slave owners attempted to dismantle the cultural traditions and memories that helped give these enslaved people their humanity. One thing the enslaved people brought, however, was something the slave owners did want them to keep: their skill working the land.

*William "Jim" Hutchinson, Jr., my grandfather*

Africans had been cultivating African rice for nearly three thousand years, along with many other crops that grow in hot regions, such as yams, black-eyed peas, peppers, okra, and watermelon. This generational knowledge carried on through enslavement, and as I got older, I found out that the Gullah Geechee people were responsible for developing irrigation systems and dams, and cultivating crops like indigo and the nationally recognized Carolina Gold rice. Known for its fluffy texture, this rice made white slave owners in Charleston some of the wealthiest in the nation. Yet enslaved Africans never saw a penny for their skill, labor, or contributions to American food.

Despite this gross injustice, and the southern American attempts to erase African culture and traditions, our ancestors resisted. The languages, traditions, culinary talent, and farming expertise that they brought with them sustained them in this new, unfamiliar place. Merging their past African life with their present American life, they began forming new ethnic traditions, which became what we know as Gullah Geechee culture. These people—my people—didn't only make the South an extremely wealthy region, we contributed a new culture and identity for an entire group of Black folks who were long told that they couldn't have one.

Historically, the Gullah Geechee people inhabited a stretch of more than 450 miles, from North Carolina's Cape Fear to Jacksonville, Florida, and today are most prominent on the Sea Islands of South Carolina and Georgia. They inhabited these islands like my ancestors did here on Edisto Island. Because enslaved Africans came from all over Africa, enslaved people were being introduced to hundreds of new African languages. These groups intermingled, found common threads, and united their native tongues and the English language into a new African creole language called Gullah. That's amazing, isn't it? Four hundred years of slavery, and the Gullah people manage to preserve African languages and heritage. Building and retaining community is how my ancestors were able to create Gullah Geechee culture, and community is how we'll make sure it survives.

For four hundred years, the Gullah Geechee people made Charleston rich through their work in the rice and indigo fields. When the Civil War broke out, everything changed. Plantation owners and Confederate generals knew a change was on the horizon. Many Gullah Geechee people, including my great-grandfather Jim Hutchinson, also known as one of the great Kings of Edisto, served in the Union Army's First South Carolina Volunteers. Many other Black Americans from South Carolina bravely served in the Union Army to fight for our freedom. As a result, enslaved Africans on the Sea Islands were among the first Black folks in the South to gain freedom. America's Reconstruction Era began, and during this time, Black people gained land, entered politics, and started building free and prosperous communities. On Edisto Island, this prosperity happened quickly thanks to several Black men and women. The Black male Edistonians who helped develop the newly freed Black community were called the Black Kings of Edisto. Thanks to their bravery, the Gullah Geechee people began a new life that wasn't in bondage through American slavery.

*My mother, Laura V. Hutchinson, with friends Margaret M. Rivers and Jim Wright. Edisto Island Community Center, 1978*

Once Black folks gained their freedom, the plantation owners and rice planters who had long inhabited the islands began to abandon their plantations. The Gullah Geechee people refused to work in rice fields that could be dangerous and disease-ridden, and many started to pursue jobs outside of the fields. My great-grandfather lived an honorable life during this time and helped many of these same Black folks find other opportunities. After serving in the Union Army, he worked in local politics, and helped newly freed Black people acquire land on this very island. He advocated for African American voting rights across the country, and organized a group of more than twenty freed Black men who collectively pooled and purchased 452 acres of island land, dividing it among Black Edistonians. Though jealousy and racism cut Jim's life painfully short, his home, built by his son Henry Hutchinson, still stands as a testament to Black Edisto's history, resilience, and love for the island. We were and are successful, and the work of Black Kings and Queens like Maum Bella, Ismael Moultrie, Alleen Woods, Doll Grant, Rev. McKinley Washington, and, of course, Jim Hutchinson created an enduring pathway for Gullah Geechee culture to survive and thrive on Edisto Island.

*Emily Meggett at Mesquite Beach in 1947, fifteen years old*

But the world has its ups and downs. On Edisto, a group of hurricanes, including the Great Storm of 1893, devastated the island. As more white people continued to leave Edisto, the Gullah Geechee people here—including my own ancestors—were able to make the land they'd developed their own, and continue developing a culture that was truly their own, unaffected by white owners. The Gullah Geechee people continued to lead successful careers in business, farming, and local leadership.

As the world continued to change in the twentieth century, so did the demographics of the southern Sea Islands. White people started to return to the region, buying up property all along the beaches. With their arrival came new development: Hotels, houses, and businesses were taking over, and the Gullah Geechee community and traditions were being ignored. As Sea Islands like Edisto Island changed, some of that history and culture was gradually ignored, and for a long time, I myself didn't know much about it.

Because of that formerly lost history, many decided to mock what they found unfamiliar. Back in the day, I might be teased for saying or pronouncing things the "Gullah" way, like calling turtles "coodahs" or saying "tenki" in place of "thanks" or "chi'ren" instead of "children." Though it's not often recognized, the Gullah people could be considered bilingual. We had to learn to speak standard English and keep our Gullah language for our home and community. When I was a child, sometimes I'd feel a little shame when people made fun of my speaking, but I learned to be proud of the way I spoke, and of my history.

Though the islands changed, we as a people prevailed, and we continue to share our histories and our stories with people just like you. Though some Sea Islands like Hilton Head and Johns Island would perhaps be unrecognizable to the people who used to live there, Gullah Geechee people have managed to preserve some of our land and culture throughout the region. There are Gullah Geechee museums across the country, festivals are held year-round to celebrate Gullah Geechee history and traditions, and leaders in the Gullah Geechee communities provide tours and talks about our history and legacy in the South. In July 2000, Gullah Geechee people came together to declare themselves a nation in front of people from all over the world, and in 2006, the United States Congress passed the Gullah/Geechee Cultural Heritage Act. This act provided $10 million over ten years to preserve historic sites in the southern Lowcountry Gullah Geechee culture. Some of the money was to be used to celebrate who we are, and preserve the stories we grew up hearing, the quilts our mothers and grandmothers made, our music, and our food.

The Gullah Geechee history and legacy have greatly impacted my own life. I grew up eating some of the same meals that my great-great-grandmother prepared in the 1840s, meals that existed even before her time. I learned early that okra—in gumbo and soup—used to be one of the most important African crops our ancestors brought here. Today, chefs and cooks all over the country use okra in their own food.

I learned that lima beans, butter beans, black-eyed peas, and other crops that we sometimes call "southern food" simply wouldn't exist without the skill and creativity of my Gullah Geechee ancestors. I learned that dishes like Charleston red rice is really Gullah red rice, thanks to our ability to grow the rice that is central to the dish, our ability to remember and redevelop African cooking traditions like one-pot rice dishes, and our introduction of the tomato base that makes this dish so loved across the Lowcountry. Now, when I grew up, I knew that these meals were our meals—meaning they were by Black people and for Black people. Okra gumbo would sustain our family during the winter, while I enjoyed red rice whenever I could. These dishes were made with what we could grow, and with meat that we could easily cook.

Bringing the skill of fishing over with us was also survivalism. Fishing and hunting were sources of free meat. So we fished and hunted because we could and also because we had to. Our relationship to the water is precious. Many enslaved Africans grew up on the West African coast, and that knowledge and history reached the southern coast of the United States. I remember my uncle Henry and my husband, Jessie, fishing in the nearby creek. They'd come back with just about everything—whiting, spottail bass, trout, flounder, mullet, different types of fish and shrimp, and even shark. We'd preserve it or cook it, and that seafood could turn into shrimp and grits with gravy (page 87), okra gumbo (page 184), or even deviled crab (page 51). These traditions are old Sea Island fishing practices, straight from the Gullah Geechee people.

I love Edisto Island very much—it's my home. But to love something or someone is to also be willing to talk about the hard things. Too much of American storytelling has ignored this country's sins. It's ignored slavery, its obsession with invalidating African culture, and its inability to recognize just how much African Americans have helped to build, develop, and shape this country. It's time to recognize the Gullah Geechee history that's part of American history. Food often tells the stories that society will not. I hope my book, and these recipes, invite you into our culture, our history, and our present. Through my cooking, I hope you enjoy the best of the South, and appreciate the Gullah Geechee influences that have made this region what it is today.

*THE 1893 STORM*

The 1893 storm came in the night. It was when my grandmother lived in the cabin on the Mitchell plantation. This is the script she wrote about it:

"The time of my life on Edisto Island where I was born. It is a small island and on this island, my father and mother live there, there were poor people work from 6 A.M. until the dawn of day. Mother & Dad were marriage in 1891. The following year, she again having children, time was harder—it seem the more kids they have the harder it got. On this plantation where they live, the master was a farmer. Mr. Mitchell had so much land until when the days is through papa get home at 9 P.M. Daddy was small. Mama & Papa, they plant a lot of corn. When it hard enough to grind they make grits, that was a big help.

In 1893 there was a big storm on this island. In this house where Mama & Papa live on this hill, not far from the river. The tide was getting higher and higher until the house was full of water. Her brother were there with her. She was praying for the tide to go down.

Instead of go down, its get worse—what ever they had was floating in the water. This house had a loft. Ma & Frank climb up there to get save. Still the tide get higher, so they went on the house top. They still surrounded by water, no house in sight.

All of a sudden the top of the house wash down, and Mama & Frank was on it from 5 P.M. until 7:30 A.M. that morning. She was out in this ocean praying and crying to be save. Rain falling, and fog on their head and shoulders. But they won't lets go the house top. That what save them.

About 6 A.M. they can see a little where they were. At 7 A.M. they foot reach sand. Where this house top tin stuck in the sand was a bundle of trees—that is where the master house was. So they walk around to the house and knock. They didn't have any clothes on but some branch they put around them.

Mr. Mitchell was shock and said what happened, Betsy what happen to your house? It all in the creek sir. How did you get here? On the house top sir.

So Mr. Mitchell put them in a little house in the yard and gave them some clothes. I don't know what was wrong with the clothes but it give Mama & Papa & Frank an itch for almost seven years after.

*—from a journal kept by my maternal grandmother, Elizabeth Major Hutchinson*

# HOW *to Use This* BOOK

WHEN I FIRST STARTED COOKIN', I MADE $11.13 PER WEEK. NOW YOU'RE READING MY COOKBOOK. HA! AIN'T THAT SOMETHIN'?

When I cook, I cook for three things: for passion, for family, and for community. That means I cook big, and I cook my memory. When I was a child, I watched Mama cook, and eventually started to cook right next to her. You never cooked just for yourself; you were always cooking for family and loved ones. I started my cooking career as a teenager in 1954 at the Dodge House. I worked in homes all over Edisto Island, and through those experiences, I didn't just learn how to cook. I learned how to cook so people would recognize your dish. Everybody knows my pink sauce; they know my fried shrimp; they know my red rice. I learned how to master recipes and make them my own.

One of the first things I learned how to make with Mama was grits. At the Dodge House, I learned how to make different types of casseroles. Now, people say that we all like different food, different spices, and things like that. Sometimes this is true, but the common thread between all groups is that we all love some good food. I learned how to make food that everyone on Edisto loves—and I mean *loves*. This came from talent and instinct, but also from learning, changing, and being willing to make mistakes and try again.

***"Good cooks don't measure. They use the imagination of the brain. Cook with the brain and heart. If you put in your heart, it will always come out good!"***

When you start cooking from my book, you'll notice some differences from most cookbooks of this day and age. First, many of my breads make two loaves, some of my soups and stews feed more than ten people, and my one-pot rice dishes can come out to two of today's "large" pots. This is because I cook big. What does that mean? Well, it means I cook the old way. Most people had large families, and I myself had ten children. Back then, many people were cooking for their families, extended relatives, church groups, and communities. This means that when I cooked, I didn't just make one cake, I made two. I made so much she crab soup that it would be multiple pots in today's cooking. I cooked so many wings, it was enough to probably serve the entire island!

Most people don't cook like that anymore, and I understand why, but I still do. In this book, I've tried to make recipes that work for four to ten people, but sometimes you're going to have a little extra. That's okay! Give a loaf of banana bread (page 244) to your neighbor. Share a bowl of oyster stew (page 179) with a friend in need. And my, oh my, if you don't share that big ol' pot of red rice (page 213) with your family? We'll have to have a little talk, now!

The second thing to know about my book is that I grew up in a generation that cooked from memory. Africans were known to pass recipes down orally, meaning they rarely wrote a recipe down on a piece of paper. This tradition carried on into the Transatlantic Slave Trade, and when African Americans started creating new dishes in the United States, they would share recipes with their children and grandchildren by mouth, not through writing. This was the way things were even when I learned how to cook. I didn't measure ingredients, I learned how to cook my dish by how it felt. If I was cooking a rice dish and I could pull the rice too easily to me, that meant the dish needed more rice. If it was too thick and heavy and difficult to move the spoon, it meant I needed to add a little more water or broth. I use my senses to cook. I feel a dish to make sure it's cooking at the right temperature or speed by using a spoon to stir a dish. I look at the stove to see if something is cooking too slowly. If I hear too much oil popping, it means something is frying too fast. I can smell my liquids to make sure they're still fresh enough for a special meal I'm cooking. And, of course, I can taste to decide if a dish needs more seasoning, more liquid, or anything else. To me, this style of cooking will go further than measurements ever can, but I know those aren't the ways of today. I provide measurements for most of these recipes, but sometimes, I leave it up to you. I encourage you to put your senses to use. If you think something needs more milk, add it! Need to take something away? That's fine too. Trust yourself. And if something doesn't work, you can always try again, just like I have.

Finally, in some of my recipe headnotes, I mention which season I usually prepare a dish. This doesn't mean this is the only season you can cook a meal. It just means that's when I tend to find the freshest ingredients for the dish. Here, where fruits and vegetables are large and plentiful, and fresh seafood and live turkeys and chicken are right down the road, we still cook food based on harvest seasons. For example, I make fried green tomatoes (page 129) in the summertime, when they're available, and I make my oyster dishes in the wintertime, when some of the best oysters are available. This is how we do things on the island. We take our directions from the land, cook what's available, and save anything we don't use for another time. Cooking by season will bring you closer to my island and its traditions.

Cooking shouldn't be scary; it should bring joy and love into your home. These recipes are meant to be enjoyed. You can swap seasonings, you can use different proteins, and you can cook things the way you want to. Don't be afraid to make my recipes your own, but always remember the history and people behind them. All these recipes are in my head and hands. I am doing this cookbook, but I don't cook by a book. I like to feel how it cooks, and cook how it feels, and if it doesn't work the first time, well, you can try it again.

Martha White
Nutrition Facts

# *Miss Emily's* ESSENTIAL KITCHEN ITEMS

IN THE WORLD I GREW UP IN, COOKING WAS A SKILL THAT REQUIRED ALL FIVE SENSES: SIGHT, SMELL, SOUND, TASTE, AND TOUCH. Recipes were usually transferred from generation to generation by word of mouth. Cooks, and even many chefs, didn't really use formal recipes and measurements in those days. Now, that doesn't mean the food wasn't good! The food was delicious, it was just made by cooks who knew how to create a good dish using their senses and their memory. One of the ways us cooks were able to remember so many dishes and methods of cooking is by using some of the same ingredients over and over again.

In my kitchen, there are several ingredients that I make sure are well stocked all the time so I can use them as many times as needed. These items range from produce to meat to powders, and all play important roles in many of my most cherished recipes. While I provide full recipes for readers, it's still important to get to know these items outside of their use in a recipe. Understanding what a vegetable should look and taste like will help you to know when it's in season in your city or town. It will also help you to think of ways to use the ingredient in your own kitchen. Having sugar on hand can help cut through some of the acid in a savory dish, and give you the base of what you need to make a perfectly sweet dessert. And that salt pork? Don't you even turn that stove on without making sure you've got some in the fridge!

One of the best things about my essential items is that they are all affordable. I didn't grow up in a wealthy home; I may not have been rich. But I knew how to make use of what I had. For most people, keeping these items in the home is actually possible. I want all people to feel like they can make my food, without having to worry about how much is in their pockets.

In my community—and certainly in my kitchen—we don't believe in waste. When cared for properly, you may use all my essential items to make many of my recipes over and over again, and to take your own approach to Lowcountry cooking, too.

∴ ∴ ∴ ∴ ∴ ∴ ∴ ∴ ∴ ∴ ∴ ∴ ∴ ∴ ∴ ∴ ∴

### BROCCOLI

Broccoli is one of the most versatile vegetables in cooking. Steamed, sautéed, or roasted, broccoli adds fresh flavor and depth to a dish, not to mention some good health benefits. I like to get my broccoli from some of my favorite neighborhood markets during the fall, winter, and spring, when the veggie is in season. Whether it's added to a dinner of rice and meat, or covered in cream sauce, its versatility means that you'll always see it in my kitchen.

### BUTTER (LIMA) BEANS

We grow butter beans, also called lima beans, right here on Edisto. I grew up eating them, and to this day, I grow them right in my garden, watching them diligently each and every day. Now, sometimes butter beans get a bad rap—folks think they're slimy and a little plain. But really, whether or not butter beans are good boils down to how they're cooked. A bit of salt pork or some seasoning will turn these beans into one of the tastiest sides you could imagine! I like cooking butter beans during the summer, but they're usually good in most seasons except the winter. The best part is that these days, you can purchase dried butter beans in stores and online. Now, you know by now that I like to grow my food, but however you get these wonderful beans is okay with me.

### CARROTS

Carrots are a special vegetable. Slightly sweet, but also a little woody, these root vegetables come in many colors—yellow, purple, and, of course, my favorite, orange. Sliced, diced, shredded, or just cut into one- to two-inch chunks, these carrots can be cooked and served in many ways. They can be served raw or cooked, and their subtle sweetness shines, whether fresh or covered in a sauce. It's good to have carrots around because you can add them to most lunch or dinner meals, and to side salads. Sometimes, I'll add a few extra carrots to a stew, or just serve baby carrots as a side. Keep a few on hand in your fridge.

### CELERY SALT

Celery salt is a mix of salt and crushed celery seeds. Like many seasoned salts, the celery taste is subtle, and helps to flavor a dish rather than overpower it. It offers that salty taste you want from a pantry seasoning, and a subtle herby flavor. Celery salt helps season dishes that benefit from some celery flavor, but don't necessarily need a full serving of celery. I call for this salt in many of my seafood dishes, and you might also use it in recipes in the poultry section, too. Celery salt is in the seasoning aisle at most grocery stores, and you can also find it online.

### CORN

Corn is a two-crop vegetable on Edisto Island. That means that we harvest fresh corn in spring and summer. Corn on the cob by itself is a wonderful treat, but you can also remove those kernels and use them in soups, stews, and as a side to chicken and meat for dinner. I love fresh corn, but I keep canned corn in my kitchen, too. Even if fresh corn is in season, there's not always a lot of time to cut corn off the cob. Having a can or two (or more) is helpful, especially when cooking Lowcountry dishes.

### COW PEAS

Cow peas are also called "southern peas." Cow peas include a number of pea varieties, including black-eyed peas, field peas, and crowder peas. These types of peas are used in southern food and soul food, and they all grow right here on Edisto Island. I use these peas for weekly dinners, and even for holidays. With some rice and meat or fish, any of these pea varieties can make a real meal. You can find cow peas in grocery stores and farmers' markets across the country.

### CRISCO

Not a lot of people use Crisco these days, but when I worked at the Dodge House, this was a key ingredient for baking cakes, pies, and more. Crisco has been around for more than one hundred years, and many desserts that we all remember from our elders probably used the shortening. To this day, I keep Crisco around so I'm always able to make something a little sweet.

### CRUSHED RED PEPPER

Heat and spice are important in southern cuisine. Crushed red pepper can heat a dish up in just one teaspoon, adding that surprising kick to stews, meats, and chicken. A little crushed red pepper goes a long way. In most of my recipes, I suggest adding this pepper based on your own tastes. Some people don't like things too spicy, and some folks like to almost cry during their meals, and both are just fine. Whatever your tastes, crushed pepper will find its way onto the dinner table.

### FLOUR (SELF-RISING AND ALL-PURPOSE)

There are two things I can't ever remember being out of: flour and sugar. In my kitchen, you'll find self-rising flour and all-purpose flour, which I use almost daily. Both of these are good for different reasons. All-purpose is almost exactly what you would think it is. It can be used to coat vegetables and seafood, to thicken up sauces, and in baking. Self-rising flour, however, is a mixture of salt, baking powder, and all-purpose flour. It's used in many of my desserts and bread dishes because it helps make these baked goods rise like they're supposed to. I prefer self-rising flour, especially White Lily brand, because it has salt and baking powder already added. I only use plain all-purpose flour for my pie crusts and a few other recipes where I list it in the ingredients. I also use self-rising flour for fried chicken, pork loins, and food that needs to brown, because plain flour does not have baking powder in it and doesn't brown as well as self-rising. I keep both types of flour on hand so I'm never in a pinch.

### GOLD MEDAL SEASONING SALT

It's always good to have a seasoning salt around that you can depend on. For me, that's Gold Medal. This red-orange seasoning blend is not as salty as some of the other seasoning salt brands, but it still adds that flavor you might need for a real large pot of veggies, or even to season meat. I have suggestions on how much seasoning salt to use in each recipe, but this is the type of seasoning you should get familiar with, so you know just how much—or how little—will create the dish you want.

### GRITS

When I would send my children off to school, they almost always went on a full stomach of grits. Grits are one of the most important and common food groups in the South. Nowadays, you'll also find colored grits. I've seen pink, red, and even blue! Grits, which come from indigenous Americans from the South, come in many forms: There's stone-ground, hominy, and, of course, regular, quick, or instant grits. Stone-ground grits are grits that have been coarsely ground between the two stones of a grits mill. They have a strong corn flavor and were the grits used by most people in the old days. Hominy grits were also more popular in the old days. People would make those by soaking dried corn kernels in an alkali solution, which would remove the rough outer hulls, creating a smooth porridge. Regular grits have a medium grind, while quick and instant grits are precooked and dehydrated. A lot of southerners might get on you for using quick or instant grits, but I won't judge!

At my house, we use the good ol' regular white or yellow grits. For as long as I can remember, we've cooked them into a porridge that can be served with seafood, beef, pork, lamb, and poultry. Grits can be fried, turned into a soufflé, or even into fried cakes. I add salt to my grits—no sugar!—and you should feel free to use whichever brand you like best.

### LONG-GRAIN WHITE RICE

Rice is the heart and soul of southern cooking. When enslaved Africans were brought to the United States, their skill with rice created grand wealth for white folks, and served as the foundation for some of the most important dishes in southern cuisine. Red rice, jambalaya, red beans and rice, and many other southern favorites simply wouldn't exist without African knowledge and skill.

There are many types of rice, but long-grain white rice is my favorite. It's the center of southern cooking, Lowcountry cooking, and Gullah Geechee cooking, and its versatility means that it can be used for just about anything. This rice is used for one-pot rice dishes, to soak up the gravy from meat and stews, and is even served at breakfast. There are many types of long-grain white rice, including jasmine rice and basmati rice. I usually use Carolina rice, which has a fluffy, light texture.

I grew up cooking my rice and rice dishes in a rice steamer. Now, I've owned my rice steamer since the 1960s. In those days, rice steamers were much bigger than those of today. There were many different ways to use them, but my way, I believe, is simple and the best. I precook my rice mixture in a pot, then transfer the precooked rice to the steamer. Once I transfer the rice, I allow the rice mixture to cook on low heat for about 20 minutes, until the water completely absorbs and you can easily fluff the rice with a fork. I've found that by using a rice steamer, the rice cooks more evenly, and it's nearly impossible to burn the bottom of the rice. While steamers aren't as common these days, I still think it's the best way to cook rice. In my recipes, I give instructions for using a regular pot as well as a steamer, but I would encourage you to use a steamer if you have one (check with your grandparents or other family elders—they might just have one on hand!). Better rice for a better dish.

### HELLMANN'S MAYONNAISE

Most people in the South swear by Duke's mayonnaise, but I like my Hellmann's. It's nothing personal, I just like the texture of Hellmann's, which is light and airy. Mayonnaise is in many of my dishes, including vegetable and meat salads. The use of mayonnaise really varies by preference. I tend to add more mayonnaise to my food because I like it to be a bit creamier and have a little weight to it, but whenever I call for mayonnaise in this book, you should adjust according to your own tastes.

### KITCHEN BOUQUET

Kitchen Bouquet may seem a little old-fashioned. You may have seen this in your grandmother's kitchen, or the kitchens of some of your elders. That's because many home cooks across the country kept this in their pantries. I still do.

I mostly use Kitchen Bouquet to brown my food, especially different types of gravy. This seasoning and browning sauce adds a deep caramel and vegetable flavor, so use it wisely. In most recipes that call for Kitchen Bouquet, I state that it's optional. It makes your food nice and pretty, so give it a try.

### NATURE'S SEASONS SEASONING SALT

This herb seasoning blend is one of my favorite pantry items. I tell ya, I have a whole case of this seasoning in the house, because I love it so much. A scented blend of salt, pepper, onion, and garlic, Nature's Seasons helps bring out the flavors of a dish, without overpowering the key ingredients of a meal. I also like this seasoning for health reasons. This seasoning blend has less sodium than most, which means I can use as much as I need to. Like celery salt, you can find it in most grocery stores, or online.

### NUTS

Any time of the year, there are always big bags of pecans and walnuts in my pantry. Nuts are very good all on their own, but I also use them to add a nutty taste and texture to breads, add balance to strong flavors like liquor in desserts, and to add a bit of heft to desserts. In most of my recipes, nuts are optional, since some folks are allergic, but if you're able to eat nuts, they are worth having in the kitchen. Crushing or breaking them can sometimes take a little bit of elbow grease (I like to use a nut grinder), but it's well worth it.

### OKRA

Okra is one of the most important imports to American cuisine. This green pod was brought to the United States by enslaved Africans—my ancestors. Okra can be traced back to the African continent and parts of South Asia. In the United States, okra is the base for gumbos, stews, and fried snacks like the southern favorite fried okra.

I prefer fresh okra to frozen okra. Even if you don't have a garden, okra is available at most farms and markets in the South during the summer. In regions outside of the South, frozen okra is available at most major grocery stores, and will work just fine in all of my recipes that call for okra.

## ONIONS

Grilled, roasted, caramelized, or even boiled, onions do it all. This vegetable has a long shelf life, and I use onion to flavor, season, and garnish a lot of my food. When I call for onions, it's typically for a white or yellow onion (yellow onions are just a bit sweeter than white), unless specified.

## POTATOES

All sorts of potatoes play a role in my kitchen. Their starchiness can help bind a seafood patty, they can function as the base of a casserole, or they can even be baked or broiled before being served with a piece of meat and vegetables. Potatoes are one of those rare pieces of produce that is perfectly delicious on its own, but adding some seasoning, using them in a savory soup of stew, or mashing them down for the holidays is where you get the real magic from these spuds.

## POULTRY SEASONING

Poultry seasoning is actually a blend of sage and thyme. This seasoning adds a strong, hearty taste to meals, and through a mix of other herbs and spices like nutmeg, rosemary, and black pepper, it adds an earthy flavor to soups, breads, and even meat rubs.

## SALT PORK

In this book, you're going to get real familiar with one of my favorite cuts of meat: salt pork. Sometimes I call this fatty, salty meat "butt's meat," which usually makes people laugh a little bit. If you come by my house, you just might leave with your own package of this goodness.

Salt pork is that good cookin', now. It adds flavor to gumbos, different types of gravy, and grains, and how it's cooked can create a lot of different flavors that can change a dish for the better. Salt pork is my favorite item to cook with, and you can learn more about this piece of meat in my full guide on page 43.

## SCALLIONS (GREEN ONIONS)

Scallions are the green cousins of onions. You can pick and choose which flavor you like best, and use them in exchange for one another, or even together. Scallions are good both cooked into dishes and as a garnish, so it's important to keep them around. You'll always be ready for whatever event you might be going to—and the dish you'll want to bring.

### SQUASH

We got some delicious squash here on Edisto, so I like to make use of it as much as I can. Squash kind of has a bad name. People don't know just how many varieties exist, and the few they do know don't get cooked the right way. There are lots of ways to use squash, depending on what kind you're using. Most of the time, I use yellow squash. They work well in a cheesy casserole, are good stuffed with a meaty mixture, and can stand alone with the right kind of seasoning.

### TOMATOES

Tomatoes are one of my favorite types of produce to grow in my garden. The fertile land here is perfect for good, juicy tomatoes, and they are at their best in the summertime. I grow red tomatoes, and I can also get green heirloom tomatoes at markets in town. Tomatoes are technically a fruit and can be used in many different ways. Red or green, you can fry them quickly, cook them low and slow in a stew, or slice them up and enjoy that juiciness on a hot summer day. However you like them, having them around will help you when you're in a pinch, and will help you cook true to how I cook here on Edisto.

### WHITE AND BROWN SUGAR

There are just some things a good cook should always have, and sugar is one of them! Of course, we know that sugar is necessary for most desserts. But sugar also has other uses, too. It helps to cut the acid in stews, and it can brighten dishes that might be too savory. You'll see sugar in dishes like my okra gumbo and tomato casserole, and sometimes I'll add another pinch of sugar for just a little more sweetness in life.

## *THE SENSATIONAL WORLD OF SALT PORK*

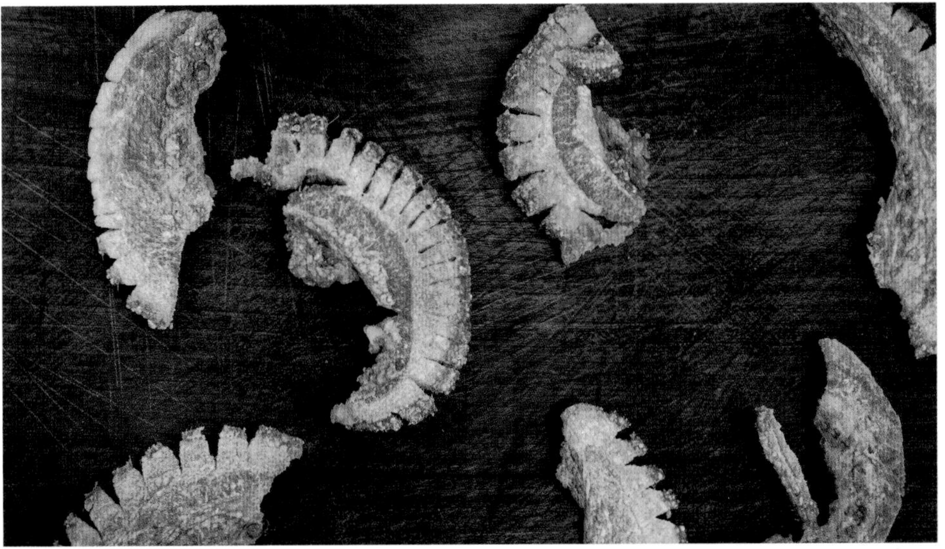

A lot of people ask me, they say, "Miss Emily? How do you get your food to taste so good?" Well, I'll tell you. There's a special meat I always use. A meat I've known since I was a child. A meat that's better than bacon (that's right, better than bacon!). It's that salt pork, and it is always in my kitchen.

Salt pork, which I also call "butt's meat," or "fatback" (not to be confused with actual fatback, which is an unsalted piece of fat with almost no meat), is a salt-cured pork that comes from the solid fat from the back of a pig (some people on Edisto call it "fatback" for that reason). This is a cut of meat that is hard fat, and it can be used to make lard. There's no skeletal muscle in this meat, just like what you would see on a charcuterie board. For us, it's not so fancy. It's just part of life.

Back when I was a child, salt pork was all I ever knew. There was no bacon when I was growing up, so this salted piece of meat came in handy. Eating salt pork was a tradition for Black folks. Every Black family had a hog and got their own meat from the hog. We'd cut that butt's meat from the hog's shoulder, where there's some of the fattiest meat on the hog. This meat was so thick, just like you would imagine a butt to be, so people ended up calling it butt's meat. They'd get that butt's meat, and they'd put it in everything. They'd fry it, they'd put it in lima beans. Just a few slices gives everything a different taste.

Salt pork is lesser known these days than it used to be, but it's still, to me, just as important. To this day, I use salt pork to add flavor to my beans, to create a thicker, more savory broth for my collard greens, and to liven up my grits and gravy. You don't need oil to fry salt pork—it makes its own flavorful drippings. Fatback can be rendered, strips can be combined with other meats to make a dish a bit saltier, and sometimes, it can even replace butter. At home, I sometimes just fry a couple of pieces of salt pork to eat as a snack, and sometimes I cook it low and slow. You can call it butt's meat, salt pork, fatback, whatever. But you know what it's really called? Good cookin'.

*"If you eat the shrimp tails, nobody knows how many shrimp you had."*

# 1 | SEAFOOD

SEAFOOD ISN'T JUST PART OF GULLAH GEECHEE CULTURE AND FOOD—IT'S THE FOUNDATION OF OUR EATING. To introduce my recipes, I'm starting with seafood, because you can't talk about Gullah Geechee cooking without talking about seafood first.

The Gullah Geechee people have a deep, historic relationship with water. A lot of people think our relationship with water begins with the horrifying journey between Africa and the Americas during American slavery, but our connection to water begins way before that, during a much more peaceful time.

Many enslaved Africans grew up on or near fishing communities and the oceanside. Researchers believe that most Gullah Geechee people descend from Sierra Leone, a coastal nation in West Africa. Our ancestors fished for seafood, just like we do today. Crab, shrimp, and fish were readily available on Africa's coast, and our ancestors were experts at fishing for what they needed for themselves and communities, without overfishing along those shores.

When our ancestors were brought here, their connection with the water was disrupted. Treacherous trips across the Atlantic Ocean, understandably, turned many enslaved people against the waters. But many Gullah Geechee people refused to let slavery's cruelty destroy our ancestral connection with the waters. We found new ways to use seafood from the American coast. We added shrimp to okra gumbo and turned crabs

OPEN
HANDICAPPED
TOWED AWAY

FLOWERS SEAFOOD
COMPANY
FRESH LOCAL
SEAFOOD
Phone: (843) 869-0033
BOILED
PEANUTS
VISA
LOCAL SHRIMP $5.99

into savory cakes. We made salmon patties, and created our own versions of she crab soup, one of the most famous dishes in Charleston.

Edisto Island is a touch of paradise. One of the island's most fruitful gifts is the abundant seafood available in our water. From the blue crabs that fill our salty seas to the whiting, carp, shrimp, and sharks found in our creeks, seafood is key to our soul, and it's what binds us together as a community. All my life, I've cooked for my family and my community, and seafood has always been part of most of those meals.

Sometimes we'd enjoy seafood with grits and gravy (page 87), and other times, we'd enjoy it during fish Fridays (page 63), a long-standing tradition in Gullah Geechee culture. My uncle Henry, who we used to call "the Creekman," would go to the creek early in the morning and come back with crab, oysters, shrimp, and clams. That fish would be so fresh and so plump, my goodness! We'd use it for everything, from okra gumbo to oyster stew. Baked, fried, or cooked down in a soup or stew, having seafood in the house meant that some good cookin' was coming up.

I cooked with seafood everywhere—in my own house and in the Dodge House, where I worked for forty-five years. She crab soup, fried shrimp, and stuffed fish with parsley rice and roe (page 71) were favorites at the Dodge House and at the other homes I worked in on Edisto Island, too. When I came home after a long workday, my children would be begging for seafood. They'd ask for fried shrimp, deviled crab, crab cakes, and shrimp and gravy. And guess what? Thanks to this island, I always had what I needed to make every single dish.

Now, back in those days, most people went straight out to the creeks to catch the fish. My husband, Jessie, and I had a system. He'd go out on Saturday morning and catch

*LEFT TO RIGHT: Emily's great-granddaughter Z'Niyah Holmes and neighborhood friends; Jamie Drayton, a fishmonger and family friend; seasoned shrimp; Emily's cousins Pakeya and Kaleb Meggett; family friend Patrick Larrymore*

as much fish as he could: whiting, bass, different types of shrimp, spottail bass, flounder, crabs, mullet, trout, and shark. He'd come back with buckets filled to the brim. He'd wash and clean the seafood, and I'd cook it up for breakfast, lunch, or dinner. I loved making Jessie his favorite, fried fish, and the kids would love it too. We'd have fried shrimp, fried oysters, and on hot summer days, Frogmore stew (page 180). And you know my rule now, don't you? There's no waste. If we had anything left over, that meant that someone who was struggling in the area could get a plate; a neighbor could take some shrimp to go. We helped each other in those days. Anybody who needed a meal knew they could come right up to my door.

You've got to learn a bit about the earth to cook the best seafood. For example, shrimp is best in March, while oysters are usually in their prime in winter, or during months that have the letter *r*. If Jessie caught too much shrimp in spring or oysters during the winter, I'd freeze them so they could last us into the coming months, and we could end up having shrimp for breakfast and dinner year-round. If he caught a lot of oysters in the fall, then we'd have a good pot of oyster stew in the winter that could feed us and all our children. Because I cook big, I'd often have food left over, even with ten children. If I made a big batch of fried shrimp or fried fish and my kids couldn't finish it, then the neighbors got some, the church members got some, everybody got some. Everybody knows that I feed the community, so if anyone was hungry or needed an extra meal for the day, they knew to come to me. The abundance of seafood on Edisto allowed me to do this for the community, and I'm grateful for it.

# Deviled Crab

SERVES: 14 TO 16

WHEN YOU ORDER DEVILED CRAB FROM RESTAURANTS IN BIGGER CITIES LIKE CHARLESTON, YOU'RE NOT GETTING THE BEST DEVILED CRAB. City folks stuff these crabs with heavy breadcrumbs and reduce the essence of the dish—the crabmeat. This here is real deviled crab—not a lot of junk. Hard work, but worth the effort.

Deviled crab is best when you kill, clean, and stuff the crab yourself, but you can find crab backs and crabmeat at the store to reduce prep time. Don't be shy with stuffing your crab back. You want that deviled crab to be overflowing so it's a real treat for guests. The Worcestershire sauce adds a light, tangy flavor, and you should add more if you like. It also doesn't hurt to be generous with your breadcrumbs. They add that subtle crunch that, when combined with the crab mixture, can take you back to memories of a sunny, sandy beach.

**10 slices white or whole wheat bread**

**3 pounds (1.5 kg) crabmeat, or about 20 blue crabs (if using prepared crabmeat, you'll also need 15 to 16 crab backs)**

**¼ cup (55 g) Nature's Seasons, or seasoning of choice**

**2 cups (250 g) diced onion**

**2 cups (200 g) diced celery**

**½ cup (1 stick/115 g) unsalted butter, plus ¼ cup (½ stick/55 g) for the crab tops**

**1 tablespoon mustard**

**½ cup (120 ml) fresh lemon juice (from 1 lemon)**

**¼ cup (60 ml) Worcestershire sauce**

**1½ cups (355 ml) mayonnaise**

Preheat your oven's broiler to 500°F (260°C) or its highest setting. On your oven's highest rack, broil all the bread slices for about 2 to 3 minutes, until golden and crisp, but not burned. Flip all the slices over and broil for another 2 to 3 minutes. Turn the broiler off and allow the bread to crisp in the oven for 15 minutes.

Remove the bread from the oven and let cool. Using a hand grater, grate the bread slices into breadcrumbs. The crumbs should look and feel like sand. Set the breadcrumbs aside.

If using fresh crabs, cook them in a large pot of boiling water with 1 tablespoon of Nature's Seasons, or your seasoning of choice. Drain, let cool, then remove the crab back from each crab. Then, remove what we call the "dead man" (the grayish crab gills; see page 59) and pick the crabmeat from the shells. Set the crabmeat aside. Clean the crab backs and save the crab bodies to stuff later.

Sauté the onion and celery in ½ cup (1 stick/115 g) of the butter over medium heat for 5 to 7 minutes, or until browned. Transfer to a medium mixing bowl, add the crabmeat, mustard, lemon juice, and Worcestershire sauce, and use a fork to stir slowly and carefully so as not to break up the crabmeat. Add the breadcrumbs to the crabmeat mixture, saving about ¼ cup for later, and toss gently.

Preheat the oven to 350°F (170°C).

Add the mayonnaise to the crabmeat mixture, and toss gently with the fork until well mixed. If the mixture is still too dry, add more mayonnaise.

Fill each crab back with the crabmeat mixture. Be generous here! Each crab back should be filled to look like a mountaintop.

After stuffing the crab backs, top each with some of the saved breadcrumbs, and add just a dot of butter to the top of each crab. Set on a baking sheet and bake for 35 to 40 minutes, until golden brown on top.

# Crab Casserole

SERVES: 10 TO 12

ON SPECIAL HOLIDAYS LIKE THANKSGIVING AND CHRISTMAS, THERE IS ALMOST ALWAYS A CASSEROLE DISH FILLED WITH THIS FLAVORFUL MEDLEY OF CRAB AND NOODLES AT OUR DINNER TABLE. And on Mother's Day, my children make this dish so I don't have to cook. I think the cream of mushroom makes the dish a little less fishy, but the sherry turns this casserole into a fancier meal—something worthy of a celebration. Fresh crabmeat is best here, but canned will work just as well.

**1 (12-ounce/340 g) box egg yolk noodles**

**2 dozen crabs, rinsed; or 2 pounds (910 g) crabmeat, undrained**

**¼ cup (½ stick/55 g) unsalted butter**

**1 small onion, grated**

**1 cup (100 g) diced celery**

**2 (10¾-ounce/298 g) cans cream of mushroom soup**

**2 tablespoons self-rising flour**

**½ cup (120 ml) half-and-half, or more if needed**

**1 cup (240 ml) milk, whole or 2%**

**¼ teaspoon ground mace**

**½ cup (120 ml) sherry**

**¼ cup (25 g) breadcrumbs**

**1 teaspoon paprika (optional)**

Preheat the oven to 350°F (170°C).

Cook the noodles according to the package instructions. Drain and set aside in a large bowl.

If using fresh crabs, fill an 8-quart (7.6 L) pot three-quarters full of water and bring to a boil over high heat. Add the fresh crabs and cook for 20 minutes. Remove the crabs from the water and allow them to cool. Remove the backs and the "dead man," the grayish gills that look like accordions (see my Removing the Dead Man guide, page 59), from each crab. Once all the backs and gills are removed, rinse the crabs. The next stage is hard work, but worth it!

Pick the meat from the back and claws. There should be about 2 pounds (910 g) meat. Add the picked crabmeat (or canned crabmeat) to the bowl of noodles and mix until combined.

In a large saucepan, melt the butter. Sauté the onion and celery in the butter over medium heat for 5 minutes. Add the cream of mushroom soup, flour, half-and-half, and milk to the saucepan and stir. If the sauce's texture is too thin, add more half-and-half as needed. Add the mace and sherry and stir. Remove from the heat.

Transfer the crabmeat and noodle mixture to a greased 9 by 13-inch (23 by 33 cm) baking dish. Pour the sauce over the crab mixture. Sprinkle the top of the casserole with the breadcrumbs and paprika, if using. Place the casserole dish in the oven, uncovered, and bake for 20 to 25 minutes, until the casserole is bubbling. Serve immediately.

# Crab Cakes

SERVES: 12 TO 14



I LIKE USING GROUND MACE—CONSIDERED THE SISTER SPICE OF NUTMEG—IN MY CRAB DISHES BECAUSE IT HELPS SHARPEN THE FLAVOR OF THE CRAB. In these rich crab cakes, you can taste the importance of mace, which is less sweet than nutmeg, but still adds a strong, peppery taste and smell. Crab cakes are fairly simple to make, but require a close eye: No one wants overly crisp or burnt cakes! The breadcrumbs should bind the cakes together, but if you find that they aren't holding together as you make them in-hand, add more breadcrumbs to your mixture by the spoonful. People often enjoy crab cakes with tartar sauce or cocktail sauce, and that's all fine and good, but you put some of my pink sauce (page 277) with these? Now you've got yourself a meal.

10 slices white or whole wheat bread

½ cup (1 stick/115 g) unsalted butter

1 large (225 g) onion, grated

¼ cup (30 g) self-rising flour

1½ cups (355 ml) milk, whole or 2%

2 large eggs, beaten

1 teaspoon fresh lemon juice

1 teaspoon distilled white vinegar

¼ teaspoon ground mace

2 pounds (910 g) lump crabmeat

½ cup (120 ml) vegetable oil, plus more as needed

Preheat your oven's broiler to 500°F (260°C) or its highest setting. On your oven's highest rack, broil all the bread slices for about 2 to 3 minutes, until golden and crisp, but not burned. Flip all the slices over and broil for another 2 to 3 minutes. Turn the broiler off and allow the bread to crisp in the oven for 15 minutes.

Remove the bread from the oven and let cool. Using a hand grater, grate the bread slices into breadcrumbs. The crumbs should look and feel like sand. Set the breadcrumbs aside.

In a large cast-iron skillet, melt the butter over high heat. Once the butter is melted, add the onion and sauté for about 5 minutes, until tender.

Pour the butter and onion into a large mixing bowl. Whisk the flour into the melted butter and onion, then slowly whisk in the milk to make a creamy sauce. Once the sauce is smooth, whisk in the eggs, lemon juice, vinegar, and mace.

In the same mixing bowl, add the crabmeat. Combine the crabmeat and cream sauce together, mixing lightly with a fork so you don't break up the pieces of crabmeat. Gently fold in just enough of the breadcrumbs so that the mixture holds together. Divide the crab mixture into equal portions (there should be 12 to 14 crab cakes). They should be thick rounds—about the size of the palm of your hand, and roughly 1½ inches (4 cm) thick.

Using your hand, take a scoop of the toasted breadcrumbs, and cover each crab cake with breadcrumbs.

Wipe out the skillet and heat the ½ cup of oil over high heat. Once the oil is hot, place a few of the crab cakes in the skillet. Reduce the heat to medium. Cook over medium heat for about 2 minutes on each side, until browned and cooked through. Working in batches, adding more oil as needed, cook the remaining crab cakes. Place the cooked crab cakes on a paper towel to drain the oil. Serve crab cakes immediately, or set aside in a warm oven (see Tip) while you cook the remaining crab cakes.

TIP: To keep the cakes warm after cooking, preheat the oven to 175°F (80°C). Place the crab cakes on a large baking sheet lined with a piece of foil and place them in the oven. At this temperature, the oven will keep them warm without drying them out.

## *REMOVING THE DEAD MAN*

In many recipes, I ask you to take a crab back off and remove the "dead man." Now, you might not know what this is, or how to do this. This guide is here to help you.

**What Is the Dead Man?**
"Dead man's fingers" are the gills of a blue crab. Where does that strange name come from? They have a grayish, shriveled appearance, which some people think makes them look like the fingers of, well, a dead man. But don't worry! Contrary to what some people believe, they are not toxic or harmful in any way. They just don't look or taste very good.

Whenever I use crabs for a recipe, I open my crabs up and remove those gills before I dig into the best part of the crab—the meat.

**Saving Crab Backs for Deviled Crab**
Place your live crab in a large pot of boiling water. Once cooked, pour the hot water off. Place the crabs in a clean sink and run cold water over them, ensuring that every crab gets some water. Once the crabs are cool, begin taking the crab back off. Take one hand and place it under the crab, on its belly. Use your other hand to pull the hard shell off of the top, or back, of the crab. If you're struggling to get it open, use a crab cracker to break the bottom shell, but be careful! You want clean, uncracked backs for your deviled crab.

Once the backs are removed from all the crabs, clean out its innards, including the dead man. Place the backs in soapy water, and wash them clean with a scrubbing pad. You'll want to wash them at least two or three times so there's no leftover crab parts or sea particles on the backs. Leave them out to dry.

Once the backs are dry, place the crab backs in a plastic bag and set them in a place for safekeeping, such as the top of your fridge or in a storage cupboard.

**Using Crabs for Frogmore Stew and Other Soups and Stews**
Place the live crab in a clean sink. Run hot water on the crabs, enough to calm them down.

Once the crabs are calm, begin removing their backs. Take one hand and place it under the crab, on its belly. Use your other hand to pull the hard shell off of the top—or the back—of the crab. If you're struggling to get it open, use a crab cracker to break the bottom shell.

Once all the backs are removed, take out their innards, including the dead man. Now, the crabs are still alive at this point, so be careful! They do pinch. To avoid a cut finger, pour some hot water over them again to calm them down as you remove the gills.

Once you've removed all of the dead man from the crabs, save the crab bodies. You will use them for the Frogmore Stew.

# Broiled Clam

SERVES: 6

MY BROILED CLAM TAKES A NIGHT TO PREP, BUT IT'S WORTH THE WAIT. Once it's time to make the clams, a few quick steps will give you piping hot shells of tender clam meat and crunchy bacon. Be careful not to overcook—the bacon should be done, but you don't want to dry out your clams. No more than five minutes of cook time will get these right where they need to be.

**2 dozen clams**

**2 slices bacon**

**Worcestershire sauce and hot sauce, to serve**

Wash all the clams well in the sink, being sure to get any sand or mud off. Freeze the clams in their shells overnight. They should be sitting in their shells, ready for their glorious table arrival the next day!

Preheat your oven's broiler to 500°F (260°C) or its highest setting. Set an oven rack 6 inches (15 cm) from the heat source.

Fill a clean sink halfway with tepid water. Remove the clams from the freezer and place them in the sink with the tepid water for about 10 minutes. The water should make the clams pop open. Using an oyster knife, finish opening any unopened or half-opened clams, and place them on a plate or in a bowl.

Line a 9 by 13-inch (23 by 33 cm) baking pan with foil. Place the clams in half shells on the baking sheet.

Cut the bacon into 24 pieces. The bacon pieces should be just long enough to fit the top of each clam. Top each clam with a piece of bacon.

Place the baking sheet under the broiler and heat for 4 to 5 minutes, until the bacon is cooked.

Serve the clams in their shells with desired amount of Worcestershire or hot sauce, or both.

# Fried Fish

SERVES: 6 TO 8

EVERY WEEK, MY HUSBAND, JESSIE, WOULD GO OUT AND FISH. He'd walk over to the nearby creek, and he would come back with overflowing buckets of fish—anything from whiting to shrimp to spottail bass, and shark—it was enough to feed half the island! Fried fish Fridays are big in our culture, so Jessie would clean the fish, and I'd cook it right up and serve it with red rice (page 213). He loved it, and my children loved it, too.

Whether you find yourself dreaming about fish (page 72) or just love that crispy, flaky taste, this fried fish recipe will carry you through Fridays, baby showers, and celebrations beyond.

**5 pounds (2.3 kg) whiting, catfish, or fish of choice**

**2 tablespoons seasoning salt**

**2 cups (480 ml) vegetable oil**

**¼ cup (30 g) self-rising flour**

**¾ cup (90 g) cornmeal**

Clean, rinse, and fillet the fish. Season the fillets with seasoning salt and set aside.

In a large cast-iron skillet, heat the oil over medium heat until shimmering.

In a brown paper bag, combine the flour and cornmeal. Place all the seasoned fish in the bag. Grip the top of the bag tightly, and shake the bag until all of the fish is well coated. Be careful to hold the bottom and top of the bag while shaking so flour and cornmeal don't leak from the bag. The key here is to bread your fish, but not too much. A few good shakes of the fish and flour should do the trick.

Once all the fish are coated, place each piece of fish in the hot oil, one by one. Make sure that the oil is very hot; otherwise, the fish will break apart.

Fry the fish over medium-high heat for about 4 minutes on each side, until golden brown. Line a plate with two paper towels. Using tongs or a large fork, place the fish on the paper towels so the extra oil can drain. Serve immediately.

# Fried Oysters

SERVES: 4

FRYING SEAFOOD CAN BE A TRICKY THING, NOW. It's a fast process, but the key is to add just enough oil, and make sure the oil is hot enough for the oysters to actually fry, instead of just soaking up the cooking oil. If you have a deep-fry thermometer, clip it to the side of the skillet and heat the oil over medium heat until the thermometer registers 350°F (170°C). If you don't have a thermometer, just drop one oyster in on its side and cook: It should be golden brown on that side within 1 minute.

Oysters are in season during the months with the letter *r*, which means they're best enjoyed during the winter. Now, since oysters are widely available, you can cook these anytime, but it's nothing like a fried oyster (or a few) during the cooler months.

**2 large eggs, beaten**

**1 tablespoon grated onion**

**⅓ cup (40 g) self-rising flour**

**1 pint (896 g) shucked oysters**

**2 cups (480 ml) vegetable oil**

**1 lemon, quartered**

**Cocktail sauce (page 276), for serving**

In a large mixing bowl, beat the eggs. Add the onion and flour, creating a batter. Set aside.

Drain the shucked oysters, and add them all at once to the batter. Mix the oysters and batter together, coating the oysters in the batter.

Pour the oil into a large cast-iron skillet. Heat the oil over high heat. There must be enough oil for the oysters to float, and the oil should be hot enough so the oysters don't sit and soak up all the oil. Once you have enough hot oil, reduce the heat to medium.

In batches, spoon the oysters into the hot oil and cook for about 1 minute on each side, until golden brown. Remove the fried oysters to a plate covered with a paper towel to drain.

Serve the oysters with the lemon quarters and cocktail sauce.

# Creamed Oyster Casserole

SERVES: 6 TO 8

MOST PEOPLE SEE OYSTERS AND THINK OF THEM AS RAW SEAFOOD. But here's the thing: Oysters can work in just about any type of meal. Here on Edisto, there are just so many oysters in our waters. Opening these fresh shells is like opening a gift—you've got a juicy, tender piece of meat sitting inside. My creamed oyster casserole always impresses, even among people who eat oysters all the time.

In this casserole, oysters are the star. You want a smooth cream sauce that doesn't drown the oysters, nor is it fully absorbed by them. The saltine crackers give this casserole a crunch, making each bite a creamy, crunchy delight. You can serve this casserole over rice, or with a biscuit or a toasted English muffin. Add a fresh green salad with fresh avocado and asparagus as another side, and you've got yourself a meal.

**¼ cup (½ stick/55 g) unsalted butter**

**1 medium onion, grated**

**2½ tablespoons all-purpose flour**

**1 cup (240 ml) whole milk**

**1½ pounds (680 g) shucked oysters**

**6 saltine crackers, crushed**

**Fresh dill or parsley, for garnish**

**Paprika, to taste**

Preheat the oven to 350°F (170°C).

In a large skillet, melt the butter over medium-high heat. Add the onion and sauté until lightly browned, 5 to 7 minutes.

Add the flour and stir. When the flour has absorbed into the butter, add the milk—a little at a time—to create a cream sauce. Don't make the sauce too loose or too thick. Add more milk if necessary.

Grease a 9 by 13-inch (23 by 33 cm) baking dish. Pour half of the cream sauce into the bottom of the dish.

Drain the oysters thoroughly of any excess water. Place the oysters in the sauce in the baking dish.

Sprinkle half of the crushed saltine crackers on top of the oysters and pour the remaining sauce over them. Sprinkle the top of the casserole with the remaining saltines.

Bake for 20 minutes. Garnish the casserole with dill and sprinkle with paprika. Serve immediately.

# Oysters on the Half Shell

SERVES: 4

OYSTERS ON THE HALF SHELL MAKE FOR A BEAUTIFUL APPETIZER THAT YOU CAN SERVE TO FAMILY AND GUESTS. I keep my recipe simple: You just need two dozen oysters to make this dish. Presentation is important here, and I recommend using Spanish moss as garnish, just like you would with parsley. If you use Spanish moss as garnish for meals during warm months, spread it out on a cookie sheet and bake at 200°F (95°C) for 10 to 15 minutes—just long enough to get rid of the red bugs. In the wintertime, cold weather kills the red bugs, so you don't need to do this process. Add some lemon for garnish, and you've got yourself one of the prettiest dishes from Edisto.

**2 dozen oysters**

**1 lemon, cut into wedges**

Clean the oyster shells thoroughly with a wire brush.

Open the oysters by placing them in the sink and running very hot water over them until the mouth of each shell opens slightly.

Open each shell with an oyster knife. Remove the oysters from the shells.

Thoroughly clean the deepest half of each oyster shell and set them aside for serving.

Place the oysters in a jar and refrigerate overnight. If time is limited, oysters can be placed in the freezer for 10 to 15 minutes.

Line a platter with Spanish moss and arrange the thoroughly cleaned oyster shells on the moss. Place 1 or 2 oysters back into each shell and garnish the platter with lemon.

# Stuffed Fish with Parsley Rice and Roe

SERVES: 6 TO 8

STUFFED SHAD IS ONE OF MY MOST RECOGNIZED DISHES. I learned how to make this at the Dodge House when I learned how to cook with new ingredients and flavors. I tell you, when shad season arrives, it's time for shad. Those Dodges would beg me for this dish. Sometimes, they'd have it every other week, and other times, I'd have to make it back-to-back, one day after another. Now, this dish is a tough guy. It takes two days to prepare and cook, and two people to put it together. Don't let that deter you, though. That shad is tender and well seasoned, the herb rice is fluffy and fragrant, and that bone broth? That's the kind of eating that'll have you set for the day.

When I make this dish, I use shad from the local fishmonger. But on Edisto, shad is only in season from about mid-February through the end of April. If you can't find shad, you can use bass, or ask your fishmonger for a similar fish—most shad are 16 to 30 inches (40.5 to 76 cm) long. To me, the most difficult part of making the shad is the deboning process. Once you get past that part, you're smooth sailing. After all that work, you'll want to make this dish real pretty. Garnish the shad and roe with a generous amount of fresh parsley and lemon.

1 (5 to 7-pound/2.3 to 32 kg) shad, or other large fish of your choice, such as bass

FOR THE BONE BROTH:

Shad (or other large fish) backbone

2 cups (480 ml) tepid water

1½ tablespoons seasoning salt, preferably Gold Medal

FOR THE PARSLEY RICE:

1½ cups (275 g) long-grain white rice

2 cups (200 g) diced celery

2 cups (250 g) diced onions

Seasoning salt, preferably Gold Medal, to taste

Nature's Seasons, to taste

¼ cup (½ stick/55 g) unsalted butter

½ cup (18 g) chopped fresh parsley

FOR THE STUFFED FISH:

¼ cup (½ stick/55 g) unsalted butter, cut into four chunks

¼ cup (30 g) self-rising flour, preferably White Lily

Paprika, to taste

Chopped fresh dill, to taste

Seasoning salt, preferably Gold Medal

2 lemons, quartered or sliced, for garnish

Fresh parsley, for garnish

FOR THE ROE (PULLED FROM SHAD OR OTHER LARGE FISH):

Seasoning salt, preferably Gold Medal

¼ cup (½ stick/55 g) unsalted butter

1 heaping tablespoon self-rising flour, preferably White Lily

½ cup (120 ml) tepid water

## A DREAM ABOUT A FISH

Have you heard the one about the dream with the fish?

In Gullah Geechee folklore, they say that when you dream about a fish, it means you or someone you know is pregnant. Now, I know that to be true. How do I know? Because it happened to me.

I dream about a fish, next thing I know, I'm pregnant! Every year I have a child, I find out because I dreamed about a fish (or a turtle—some kind of water creature). Now, I love my kids, but when I had those fish dreams, my goodness! I knew I was in for something new.

*ABOVE: Cooking with my great-granddaughter, Denise Ravenel*

Preheat the oven to 350°F (170°C).

Rinse the shad and pat it dry with a paper towel. Remove the roe from the shad and set aside.

Remove the backbone of the shad without breaking the skin on the back of the fish. When the backbone is removed, the fish will lay out flat. Set the backbone aside.

Debone the shad, one side at a time. It's almost impossible to take out all of the bones, but you want to remove as many as possible. This process takes about 30 minutes.

Rinse the deboned fish with cold water. Season the fish with seasoning salt. Set aside.

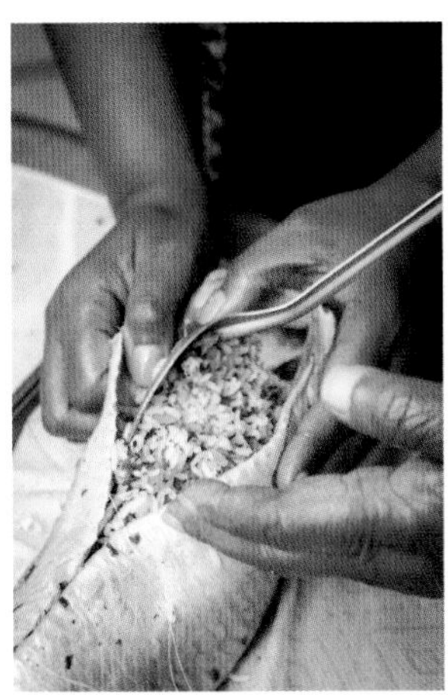

**MAKE THE SHAD BONE BROTH:** In a large, 4-quart (3.8 L) pot, put the backbone of the shad in the water and season with seasoning salt to your liking. Bring to a boil and cook on medium heat for 10 minutes. Remove the backbone from the broth with either a spoon or a mesh strainer and discard the bone, and remove the pot from the stove. Set the broth aside.

**MAKE THE PARSLEY RICE:** Bring the rice and water to a boil according to the package instructions. Add the butter, and cook until the water is absorbed. Once the rice is done, stir in the parsley. Set the rice aside.

In a 10-inch cast-iron skillet, melt ½ stick (55 g) butter over medium heat. Once melted, add the celery and onions and sauté for 3 to 5 minutes, until tender. Add the parsley.

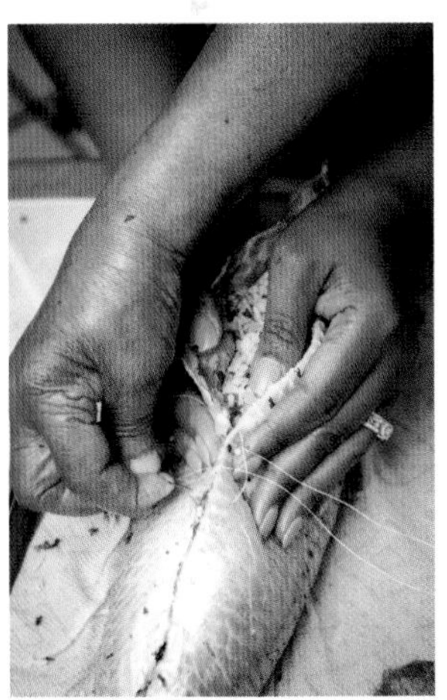

Remove the skillet from the heat. Add the sautéed onion mixture to the rice, folding it in gently, and season to taste with Nature's Seasons.

**MAKE THE STUFFED FISH:** Open the fish. Using a spoon, fill the cavity of the fish with the parsley rice.

Ask a friend or helper to grab the fish on both sides and close the fish, so the rice is completely inside. This person needs to continue holding the fish together.

Using a large needle and regular white thread, sew the fish back together while the helper holds the fish.

Get a baking dish or baking pan that can fit the fish you've decided to use.

Get a piece of aluminum foil that's large enough to wrap around the entire fish. Cover the baking dish with the aluminum foil. Coat the foil with 1 tablespoon of the butter.

Dust both sides of the stuffed fish with the flour. Sprinkle the fish with paprika, dill, and seasoning salt to taste.

Lay the fish on the buttered foil and place the remaining three pieces of butter on the top of the fish.

Pour at least ⅓ cup (75 ml) of the fish bone broth into the foil wrap as you're closing it around the fish. Seal the foil and pour the remaining broth into the pan around the foil in order to keep the pan from burning.

Place the pan in the oven and bake for 45 to 60 minutes. You can open up the foil just slightly to check if the fish is browned and determine when the fish is cooked. You may check by inserting a clean fork in the middle of the fish and ensuring that it's flaky.

When the fish is done, remove it from the oven. Heat the broiler to 500°F (260°C) or to your broiler's highest setting. Open the foil, and place the fish under the broiler to brown, about 10 minutes.

**WHILE THE FISH IS BAKING, MAKE THE ROE:** Rinse the roe and season with seasoning salt.

In a 10-inch cast-iron skillet, melt the butter over medium-high heat.

Lightly sprinkle flour on both sides of the roe. Place the roe in the skillet and fry for 4 to 6 minutes, browning both sides.

Add the water to the skillet and simmer until the roe is cooked and slightly crisp, but not burned 20 to 25 minutes.

Serve the stuffed fish with parsley rice and roe immediately, garnished with parsley sprigs and lemon.

# Fish Cakes

SERVES: 6 TO 8

THESE FISH CAKES ARE A LOT LIKE SALMON PATTIES (PAGE 83). They are real easy to make, and can fill you up on a busy day. You can use fresh fish or leftover fish to make this dish.

**6 slices white or whole wheat bread**

**1 pound (455 g) grouper, flounder, or snapper**

**1 potato, diced**

**1 onion, grated**

**1 large egg, beaten**

**Nature's Seasons, to taste**

**⅓ cup (80 ml) vegetable oil**

Preheat your oven's broiler to 500°F (260°C) or its highest setting. On your oven's highest rack, broil all the bread slices for about 2 to 3 minutes, until golden and crisp, but not burned. Flip all the slices over and broil for another 2 to 3 minutes. Turn the broiler off and allow the bread to crisp in the oven for 15 minutes.

Remove the bread from the oven and let cool. Using a hand grater, grate the bread slices into breadcrumbs. The crumbs should look and feel like sand. Set the breadcrumbs aside.

In a large, 8-quart (7.5 L) pot, bring 4 quarts (3.8 L) water to a boil over high heat. Add the fish and boil until cooked.

Once the fish is cooked, drain the fish. Remove the skin and bones.

In a 4-quart (3.8 L) saucepan, bring 2 quarts (2 L) water to a boil over high heat. Add the potato and cook until it's soft. Drain. Using a large spoon or potato masher, mash the potatoes.

In a large mixing bowl, combine the cooked fish, potato, onion, and egg. Season the mixture with Nature's Seasons.

Divide the fish mixture into equal portions. The size is up to you, but I usually like mine as thick rounds—about the size of the palm of your hand, and roughly 1½ inches (4 cm) thick.

Using your hand, take a scoop of the toasted breadcrumbs, and cover each fish cake with breadcrumbs.

In a large cast-iron skillet, heat the oil over high heat. Working in batches, drop the fish cakes into the oil. Cook until golden brown, about 1 minute on each side. Remove to paper towels to drain, then serve hot.

# Creole Shrimp

SERVES: 4 TO 6

IN SOUTH LOUISIANA, MANY DISHES USE WHAT'S CALLED THE "HOLY TRINITY." The holy trinity—onion, bell pepper, and celery—is a big part of Cajun cuisine and Louisiana creole cooking. My creole shrimp use this holy trinity, and like many creole dishes, the herb smell that fills the kitchen during cooking is just as wonderful as the taste of the shrimp once they reach the plate. The bacon adds a rich, crispy texture, while the tomatoes serve as the fresh base for this wonderful sauce. Shrimp cooks quickly, so be careful to sauté only until pink. Serve creole shrimp over a bed of white rice.

**5 slices bacon**

**1 large onion, finely chopped**

**1 bell pepper, finely chopped**

**1 cup (100 g) diced celery**

**2 garlic cloves, finely chopped**

**10 small tomatoes (2 pounds/910 g), peeled and diced**

**2 teaspoons sugar**

**¼ cup (½ stick/55 g) unsalted butter**

**2 pounds (910 g) shrimp, peeled and deveined**

**Seasoning salt, preferably Gold Medal, to taste**

**Cooked long-grain white rice, for serving**

In a 10-inch (25 cm) cast-iron skillet, cook the bacon over medium-high heat until crisp. Remove from the heat and let cool. Cut the cooled bacon into small pieces. Set aside.

In the skillet, cook the onion, bell pepper, celery, garlic, tomatoes, and sugar for at least 1½ hours over low heat. This mixture needs to "cook down," which means that the sauce needs to thicken and shrink. The consistency should be a thick sauce, similar to a spaghetti sauce.

About 5 minutes before the mixture finishes cooking, melt the butter in a small skillet. Add the shrimp and cook over medium heat until pink, 1 to 2 minutes.

Drain the shrimp. Add the shrimp and cooked bacon to the tomato mixture. Add Gold Medal seasoning salt. Taste, and add more as needed. Stir, and serve over white rice.

# Curried Shrimp

SERVES: 6 TO 8

WHEN I WORKED FOR THE DODGE FAMILY, I WAS ABLE TO COOK WITH A LOT OF INGREDIENTS FROM OTHER PLACES THAT WE DIDN'T REALLY USE ON EDISTO. Curry was one of them. It's known for its strong scent, but it's that subtle sweetness in the earthy spice that makes this such a special powder to cook with. In this recipe, I use tomato paste to deepen the orange color from the curry and add an even richer flavor. I also top this dish with peeled, diced apples, adding an irresistible crunch to this lovely lunchtime meal. As my friend Becky Smith always says, "Now, Em, this is some really good cookin' here."

**1 pound (455 g) small shrimp**

**½ cup (1 stick/115 g) unsalted butter**

**¼ cup (30 g) self-rising flour, preferably White Lily**

**1½ teaspoons Nature's Seasons**

**2 cups (480 ml) plus 2 tablespoons whole milk**

**1 cup (240 ml) half-and-half**

**1 tablespoon tomato paste**

**2 tablespoons curry powder**

**Cooked long-grain white rice, for serving**

**1 Red Delicious apple, peeled and diced, for serving**

Peel, wash, and devein the shrimp. Remove the tails. Set the shrimp aside.

In an 8-quart (7.5 L) pot, boil about 2 quarts (2 L) water. Place a large steel bowl on top of the pot, making sure the bottom of the bowl doesn't touch the water. If you have a double boiler, you may use that instead.

In the large mixing bowl, make a cream sauce. Melt ½ stick (55 g) of the butter. Once melted, whisk in the flour, Nature's Seasons, milk, and half-and-half. Reduce the heat and cook for about seven minutes.

In a separate, large skillet, add tomato paste. Sauté the tomato paste over medium-high heat for 3 minutes, being careful not to burn the paste. Add the curry powder and sauté together. Pour this mixture into the double boiler or steel bowl and mix until combined. Reduce the heat to low.

In a separate pan, melt the remaining ½ stick (55 g) butter over medium-high heat. Add the shrimp and sauté until the shrimp turns pink, about 5 minutes.

Remove the shrimp from the pan. Add the shrimp to the cream sauce and mix well.

Serve the curried shrimp over white rice. As you're serving, add a few diced apples to each plate.

# Fried Shrimp

SERVES: 10 TO 12

IF YOU GO TO ONE OF THESE RESTAURANTS IN THE CITY, THEY HAVE FRIED SHRIMP ON THE MENU. But the fried shrimp they give you aren't the real fried shrimp, the good fried shrimp. They are tiny shrimp, dipped in heavy batter, and are mostly just a lot of bread with little taste of seafood. Not my shrimp.

My fried shrimp are covered in just enough flour to give them a light, crunchy fried layer. I use medium-sized shrimp, which aren't as easily drowned out by oil and breading as the shrimp you find in restaurants. It seems like any time I made fried shrimp, everyone on the island somehow knew. I'd make a big batch so I could serve my family and anyone who stopped by. This recipe will give you plenty of shrimp, enough for family, guests, and anybody who "just happens" to stop by. And *if you eat the shrimp tails, nobody knows how many shrimp you had.*

I always serve these with my cocktail sauce (page 276) or pink sauce (page 277).



**3 pounds (1.4 kg) medium-sized shrimp**

**Gold Medal seasoning salt, to taste**

**2 large eggs, beaten**

**1 cup (240 ml) milk, whole or 2%**

**2 cups (250 g) self-rising flour, preferably White Lily**

**2½ cups (600 ml) vegetable oil, plus more as needed**

Peel, devein, and wash the shrimp, leaving the tails attached. Drain the shrimp in a colander.

Season the shrimp with seasoning salt to taste and place in a bowl.

In a separate, medium mixing bowl, mix the eggs and milk with a fork. Pour over the shrimp.

Pour the flour into a brown paper bag. By hand, dip out enough shrimp for the first batch of frying and drop them into the bag. Be sure to flour the shrimp as they are cooked, not all at once.

Close the top of the bag and shake the bag until the shrimp are coated.

In a cast-iron skillet, heat the oil until very hot but not smoking.

Place the shrimp in a single layer in the skillet and fry for 3 to 5 minutes. Do not overcook! Shrimp are easy to overcook. Drain the shrimp on a plate lined with a paper towel.

Repeat this process until all the shrimp are fried, then serve immediately.

# Garlic Shrimp

SERVES: 4 TO 6

GARLIC SHRIMP IS AN EASY DISH THAT HOLDS A LOT OF FLAVOR. Parsley or chives work well here and add balance to the dish so the garlic isn't too overwhelming.

**3 pounds (1.4 kg) medium shrimp**

**½ cup (1 stick/115 g) unsalted butter**

**3 garlic cloves, or more or less to taste, crushed**

**1 teaspoon Gold Medal seasoning salt, plus more to taste**

**1 teaspoon chopped fresh parsley and/or chives**

**Cooked long-grain white rice and garlic bread, for serving**

Wash, peel, and devein the shrimp. You may keep the tails or remove them, according to preference. Set aside.

In a medium cast-iron skillet, melt the butter over high heat. Adjust the stove's temperature to medium heat and add the crushed garlic. Cook for 4 minutes.

Add the shrimp. Sauté the shrimp over medium heat for 3 to 4 minutes, until pink.

Season the shrimp with seasoning salt to taste. Garnish with parsley, chives, or both. Serve over white rice with garlic bread.

VARIATION: If desired, make a sauce for the shrimp: Just after adding the shrimp to the skillet, sprinkle 1 teaspoon flour over the shrimp and stir in ⅓ (75 ml) water. Mix it together—it gives you a gravy.

# Salmon Patties

MAKES: 6 TO 8

SALMON PATTIES ARE ALMOST IDENTICAL TO FRENCH SALMON CROQUETTES. It's another example of the French influence on Lowcountry cuisine. Salmon patties are cherished in Gullah Geechee cuisine. People call them salmon patties, salmon cakes, and salmon patty. What connects them all are the inexpensive ingredients that shape this fried fish cake. I serve my salmon patties with grits, and you can also enjoy them with a fresh salad.

**1 onion, grated**

**2 large eggs**

**1 (14¾-ounce/418 g) can pink salmon**

**1 heaping tablespoon flour**

**1½ teaspoons seasoning salt, preferably Gold Medal**

**¼ cup (25 g) breadcrumbs, toasted**

**½ cup (120 g) vegetable oil**

In a large mixing bowl, mix the onion and eggs together. Once combined, add the salmon, flour, and seasoning salt. Stir well to combine.

Divide the mixture into equal portions. They patties should be thick circles—about the size of the palm of your hand, and roughly 1 to 1½ inches (2.5 to 4 cm) thick.

Using your hand, take a scoop of the toasted breadcrumbs, and cover each salmon patty with breadcrumbs.

In a large cast-iron skillet, heat the oil over medium-high heat. Once the oil is shimmering, working in batches if necessary, drop the patties into the hot oil. Reduce the heat to medium and cook the patties on one side until golden brown, 3 to 5 minutes, then turn and cook until the other side is golden brown. Place on a paper towel to drain.

# Shrimp and Macaroni Salad

SERVES: 8 TO 10

ONE DAY, I WANTED TO MAKE A SEAFOOD DISH BUT REALIZED I DIDN'T HAVE ENOUGH SHRIMP. Instead of letting the shrimp go to waste, I cooked a few macaroni noodles, put the two together, and created a salad that my children loved. This dish comes together quickly, and you can serve it warm or cold with a green salad and hot biscuits (page 214).

**2 pounds (910 g) shrimp, preferably small**

**1 (16-ounce/455 g) box macaroni noodles, cooked according to package instructions**

**6 hard-boiled eggs, roughly chopped**

**3 tablespoons sweet pickle relish**

**1 cup (100 g) diced celery**

**1 cup (240 ml) Hellmann's mayonnaise**

**2 tablespoons mustard**

**2 teaspoons celery salt**

Peel, wash, and devein the shrimp. Remove the tails.

In a 4-quart (3.8 L) saucepan, bring 3 cups (720 ml) tepid water to a boil and add the shrimp; cook until pink and opaque throughout, 2 to 4 minutes. Drain and set aside.

In a large bowl, combine the macaroni, shrimp, eggs, relish, and celery. Add the mayonnaise, mustard, and celery salt and mix again. Serve immediately or chill in the refrigerator and serve cold.

# Shrimp and Grits with Gravy

SERVES: 8 TO 10

SHRIMP AND GRITS IS ONE OF THE MOST RECOGNIZED DISHES OF LOWCOUNTRY COOKING. While it became popular in southern restaurants during the 1980s, shrimp and grits has roots in indigenous American foodways and West African cooking traditions. Like our African ancestors who would often include a starch with a meal, the Gullah Geechee people would put shrimp and grits together to start the day. Little did those people know that the dish would become a southern brunch staple.

My recipe for shrimp and grits is an ode to my childhood memories of eating shrimp and gravy with grits on this beautiful island. Grits was the first dish I made with Mama, and I carried that tradition into motherhood. As a mother, I woke up at 4:00 a.m. and had to have breakfast ready for my husband and children before we all went to work or school. I would prepare these shrimp and grits because the gravy—flavorful as it is—comes together very quickly. I like to brown my gravy with Kitchen Bouquet, but back in the old days, if it wasn't available, we used to add a teaspoon of instant coffee or a little leftover coffee to create the brown color for gravy.

While shrimp and grits is traditionally eaten during the breakfast hour, you can enjoy this meal anytime, anyplace.

**¼ pound (115 g) salt pork, cut into 4 (1-inch/2.5 cm) slices; or 6 slices bacon, cut into 1-inch (2.5 cm) pieces**

**1 onion, chopped**

**½ cup (95 g) self-rising flour, preferably White Lily**

**5 cups lukewarm water, plus more if needed**

**2 cups (340 g) regular grits**

**¼ cup (½ stick/55 g) unsalted butter**

**4 pounds (1.8 kg) medium shrimp, peeled and deveined, tails removed**

**1 teaspoon seasoning salt, preferably Gold Medal, plus more to taste**

**Crushed red pepper**

**1 teaspoon Kitchen Bouquet (optional)**

In a large skillet, fry the salt pork or bacon over medium heat for 5 to 7 minutes, until slightly crunchy. (You do not need cooking oil; the salt pork makes its own drippings.) Add the onion and sauté with the salt pork or bacon until softened, 5 to 7 minutes.

Slowly add the flour, using a spoon to combine it with the sautéed pork and onion. Once all the flour is added, use a spoon to mix the ingredients together. Stir constantly, while slowly adding the water and creating a gravy; cook for about 10 minutes.

Adjust the heat to high and allow the mixture to come to a boil, cooking until thickened. Cook for 3 to 5 minutes longer to remove the flour taste. Adjust the heat to low.

Meanwhile, prepare the grits according to the package instructions and set aside.

In a separate skillet, melt the butter over medium-high heat. Add the shrimp and cook until they turn pink, 2 to 3 minutes. Remove the shrimp from the butter and add them to the gravy. Season with seasoning salt and crushed red pepper to taste. Add the Kitchen Bouquet, if using.

Top the prepared grits with the shrimp gravy and serve.

# Shrimp Salad

SERVES: 6 TO 8

SHRIMP SALAD IS A WONDERFUL FRESH DISH FOR THE WARMER MONTHS. Shrimp salad offers a taste of the beach and, like chicken salad, is perfect for picnics, large lunches, and an afterschool snack for kids. If you're preparing this for a special event, you can stuff hollowed-out tomatoes or bell peppers with it for a beautiful presentation.

**3 pounds (1.4 kg) small or medium shrimp**

**1 cup (100 g) chopped celery, covered with ice water and refrigerated overnight for crispness**

**1 scallion**

**4 hard-boiled eggs, chopped**

**½ to 1 cup (120 to 240 ml) mayonnaise, preferably Hellmann's**

**1 to 2 tablespoons mustard**

**Celery salt, to taste**

Peel, wash, and devein the shrimp. Remove the tails. Bring 8 cups (1.9 L) water to a boil over high heat. Add the shrimp and boil until they turn pink, 2 to 3 minutes. Drain and allow the shrimp to cool. Set aside.

Drain the celery. Place the celery on a paper towel and pat dry.

In a large mixing bowl, combine the shrimp, celery, spring onion, boiled eggs, mayonnaise, and mustard to taste. Add celery salt to taste and stir. Refrigerate to chill. Serve.

# Shrimp Rice

SERVES: 10 TO 12

SHRIMP RICE IS A VERY SIMPLE DISH TO MAKE, BUT IT PACKS THE FLAVOR. When you cut your bacon, the slices should be no bigger than a fingertip, and you want your onions chopped fine.

**2 pounds (910 g) small shrimp**

**6 slices bacon**

**1 large onion, diced**

**¼ cup (½ stick/55 g) unsalted butter**

**1 tablespoon seasoning salt, preferably Gold Medal**

**1 teaspoon crushed red pepper**

**3 cups (555 g) long-grain white rice, rinsed**

Peel, devein, and wash the shrimp. Remove the tails. Set aside.

In a large skillet, cook the bacon for about 5 minutes, or until crisp, and chop it into small pieces. Add the onion and cook it with the bacon for 3 to 5 minutes, allowing the onion to become coated with bacon fat.

In a separate pan, melt the butter over medium-high heat. Add the shrimp and cook until pink, 2 to 3 minutes. Remove the cooked shrimp from the butter and add it to the skillet with the bacon and onion. Add 4½ cups (1 L) tepid water along with seasoning salt and crushed red pepper. Bring the water to a boil, then add the uncooked rice. Cook over low heat, stirring frequently, until the rice has absorbed almost all of the water, 15 to 20 minutes. Stir with a fork to ensure the rice is fluffy and done.

BUY LOCAL
ICECREAM
WELCOME
to our
FARM
GEORGE AND PINK'S
Farm & Market
Farm Fresh
Vegetables
SPRING & SUMMER HOURS
Monday - Saturday 8am-6pm
Sunday 1pm - 6pm
Pimento cheese
Callies Biscuits
Geechie Boy Products
Blenheim Gingerale
Broccoli
Boiled Peanut
Charleston TEA
OPEN
AT 1:00PM
ON
Sunday

# 2 | VEGETABLES & SIDES

BACK THEN, THERE WERE CROWDER PEAS, OKRA, BUTTER BEANS, BLACK-EYED PEAS, TOMATOES, SWEET POTATOES, CORN, SQUASH, AND MUSCADINES. These are just some of the fruits and vegetables we'd grow right in our garden when I was growing up on Edisto Island.

CHAPTER 2

Farming and gardening runs in our blood. Gullah Geechee heritage was built around our relationship to the land, from our love of sea and earth to our personal, spiritual relationship with the growing process behind the best fruits, vegetables, and grains. Mama worked at a place called the Mitchell Place Plantation, where she used to plant sweet potatoes and corn. During my teenage years, I started thinking about what kind of work I would do in my life. I knew I didn't want to work in the fields like my family did, but I did want to grow fruits and vegetables for my family, and for myself.

I've had gardens all over this island, from the one that used to be at the house where I was raised, to the vegetable garden that I used to tend to with my cousin Maurice, to the garden I look over every day right in my backyard. I know it's easy to get vegetables from the market, and sometimes I do! My friends at King's Farm Market and George & Pink always have some of the island's best produce. But I tell ya, now, there's nothing like picking tomatoes from your garden to make a salad, or using garden field peas to make hoppin' John for New Year's, or growing okra for large pots of okra gumbo and okra soup, or bites of fried okra. Growing your own food doesn't just give you better dishes. It's an opportunity to connect to the earth like our ancestors did—through mind, body, and spirit.

Since produce is now mass-produced, you can make a lot of these recipes year round. But I still like to cook according to when a fruit or vegetable is in season. If you do decide to use fresh produce, make sure to pay attention to the season label under each recipe. It will help you make the best possible dish for you and your community. And of course, always wash your produce—whether from the grocery store or your own garden—before using in any recipe.

I can't talk about produce without talking about Gullah Geechee history in this country. Slavery corrupted our ancestors' relationship with the earth. When our ancestors first arrived, they didn't grow produce for fun, they grew produce for survival. White enslavers relied on our ability to grow crops for their businesses and for their families. Enslaved Gullah Geechee people often relied on their own gardens to feed themselves, since slave owners usually only offered scraps, or the worst of their food. Backbreaking labor that lasted from sunup to sundown made many of our people desert anything to do with the land. I don't blame them. They were forced to work under horrific conditions, including long days under the sun, threats of beatings, and a complete lack of care for their health and well-being.

But we must remember our history beyond slavery. Before we were American, before we were enslaved, we were a people with an identity and culture that worked in collaboration with the earth, and benefited from its offerings. We cared for the land, and it cared for us. Throughout my life, I've honored this history by caring for any land that I've lived on or owned. I've planted, grown, and cooked food for everyone using the best of what Edisto's earth has to offer. These recipes reflect this lifelong journey, and my love of what the earth continues to give us.

# Fried Okra

SERVES: 6 TO 8

DURING ENSLAVEMENT, AFRICANS BROUGHT OVER MANY CROPS, INCLUDING OKRA. Okra has become the base for a lot of American favorites, like gumbos, stews, and the bite-sized delights that we know as fried okra. You can find fried okra all over the South, but the Gullah Geechee people on the Sea Islands keep the dish close to us, finding our own special ways to make it at home for our families and communities.

Okra is in season during the summer, which is when I really love to make my fried okra. Because these bites are so delicious, it's easy to eat an entire batch in one sitting. But you can easily serve these little fried pods with fried chicken (page 149), fried shrimp (page 80), or any baked meat. I like to taste the okra in my fried okra, so I don't cover mine in too much cornmeal, nor do I fry it for too long. You want to use fresh okra for this dish, so you get a clean, fresh-tasting fried treat. You can find fresh okra at farmers' markets and local shops, and I tell ya', you'll be glad that you got the real stuff.

**4 cups (620 g) okra**

**1½ tablespoons salt, plus more to taste**

**1½ cups (340 g) yellow cornmeal**

**2 cups (480 ml) vegetable oil**

Wash the okra. Cut the okra crosswise into 1/2-inch (1.25 cm) pieces and place in a large bowl. Season the okra with salt, adding more to taste.

Pour the cornmeal over the okra. Using both hands, firmly grip the bowl, and shake it until all the okra pieces are coated. If too dry, a little water and more cornmeal can be added.

Lightly press the okra with your hands, making sure that the cornmeal sticks to the okra. Toss the okra again. All the pieces should be coated evenly, but be careful not to use too much batter.

In a large cast-iron skillet, heat the oil over high heat. Make sure the oil is at 350°F (170°C). If it's not hot enough, the okra will soak up the oil. Dropping a pinch of cornmeal into the oil will tell you if the oil is ready to fry. The oil should sizzle, but not smoke.

Once the oil is ready, drop the okra pieces in batches into the hot oil. Cook the okra in the hot oil for about 5 minutes. The hot oil will keep the cornmeal on the okra. Once golden and crisp, remove to a plate covered with a paper towel to drain excess oil. Serve immediately.

# Beets

SERVES: 6 TO 8

I LOVE BEETS, AND I THINK PICKLING THEM IS ONE OF THE BEST WAYS TO BRING OUT THEIR STRONG, earthy flavor. I usually make this dish in the wintertime, when beets are in season. Their sour taste shines here, and just a bit of sugar tempers the veggie's bitter taste.

**1½ pounds (680 g) beets, sliced into ¼-inch (6 mm) rounds**

**8 cups (1.9 L) water**

**2 tablespoons cornstarch**

**3 tablespoons cider vinegar**

**2½ tablespoons sugar**

**¼ cup (½ stick/55 g) unsalted butter**

Clean—but do not peel—the beets.

In an 8-quart (7.5 L) pot, bring the water to a boil over high heat. Once boiling, reduce the heat to medium. Add the beet slices to the pot and cook over medium heat until tender, about 30 minutes. Drain the beets and save the beet water. Set the beets aside.

In a large pot, combine the cornstarch and a little of the beet water, making a slurry.

Add the remaining beet water to the slurry mixture, and heat over medium heat. The mixture should thicken, resembling the texture of a sauce or paste. Once thickened, stir in the vinegar, sugar, and butter. Return the beets to the pot and stir well. Remove from the stove and serve the beets with the juices from the pot.

# Crowder Peas, Black-Eyed Peas, or Cowpeas

SERVES: 8 TO 10

MANY PEOPLE ARE FAMILIAR WITH BLACK-EYED PEAS, BUT NOT CROWDER PEAS (NOT TO BE CONFUSED WITH BLACK-EYED PEAS). While crowder peas come from the same family as black-eyed peas, crowder peas are slightly bigger, and they don't have that notorious black eye. Crowder peas are Black folks' food—they sustained enslaved people in the South, and they sustained us growing up. We learned how to bring out the best of their flavor—the saltiness of pork mixes well with the starchiness of the peas—and thankfully, those techniques can be applied to whichever peas you have available. Because crowder peas are hard to find outside of the Lowcountry, you can use black-eyed peas or cowpeas for this recipe. Whichever you choose, make sure to wash your peas thoroughly to remove dirt and stones, and purchase the best ham hocks you can, as they give a salty and meaty flavor that you just can't resist.



**2 (14-ounce/400 g) smoked ham hocks sliced into 1-inch pieces**

**1 quart (660 g fresh or 898 g dried) fresh or dried crowder peas, black-eyed peas, or cowpeas**

**1½ tablespoons salt, plus more if needed**

**1½ teaspoons pepper, plus more if needed**

In a large, heavy-bottomed pot, combine 3 quarts (2.8 L) tepid water and ham hock chunks. Cook over medium-low heat for about 45 minutes.

While the ham hocks are cooking, wash the peas thoroughly, removing any dirt or stones. About 30 minutes into cooking the ham hocks, add the peas to the pot, bring to a boil, and boil for about 5 minutes. Reduce the heat to medium and cover the pot. If using fresh peas, cook for about 1½ hours. If using dried peas, cook for 2 to 2½ hours.

Season with salt and pepper to taste.

TIPS: The liquid in the finished pot of peas should be a gravy consistency, not watery.

When working with peas/beans, canned peas/beans require the least amount of cooking time—about 15 minutes, followed by green or frozen peas/beans, which require 45 minutes. Fresh-from-the-garden peas need 1½ hours.

Dried peas/beans require the longest cooking time, 2 to 2½ hours. Bring them to a boil, then reduce to medium heat and simmer until done. Add water and cook longer as needed.

# Butter Beans

SERVES: 4 TO 6

BUTTER BEANS, ALSO KNOWN AS LIMA BEANS, GROW IN ABUNDANCE ON EDISTO ISLAND. Now, some people see butter beans as too slimy or strange, but they don't realize how delicious these beans are once you add some good meat, like bacon, ham, or my favorite, salt pork. We used to grow them in our gardens. We'd eat a bunch of them during the summer and save any extra for later in the year. These beans go with a lot of meals, but I especially like to eat them with chuck roast (page 161) and a side of white rice.

**2 cups (340 g) dried butter beans**

**4 cups (960 ml) water**

**1 slice salt pork, bacon, or ham**

**1 teaspoon Nature's Seasons, plus more to taste**

Wash the butter beans thoroughly, removing all stones and dirt. In a large, heavy-bottomed pot, combine the water, salt pork, Nature's Seasons, and butter beans.

Cook the butter beans on medium-high heat for about 1 hour, or until the beans are tender.

Stir and taste the beans, and add more seasoning if needed. Serve immediately.



# Carrot Salad

SERVES: 4 TO 6

SIMPLE AND SWEET, GRATED CARROT SALAD IS A GREAT SIDE DISH. I usually serve this in the fall when a lot of the island's red apples are in season.

**6 carrots, grated**

**⅓ cup (50 g) raisins**

**1 red apple, diced**

**¾ cup (180 ml) mayonnaise**

In a large mixing bowl, combine the carrots, raisins, apple, and mayonnaise. Stir the ingredients together and serve immediately.

# Broccoli with Cheese Sauce

SERVES: 6 TO 8

YOU CAN USUALLY FIND GOOD BROCCOLI YEAR-ROUND, BUT I LOVED MAKING THIS DISH DURING THE FALL MONTHS WHEN IT WAS READY TO HARVEST. You want to search for heads of broccoli that have small florets tightly packed in together. Of course, make sure the broccoli is green, and that you don't see any yellowing (this means the broccoli is on its last leg). Fresh broccoli is best here, but you can also use frozen broccoli, or even fresh cauliflower.

**3 stalks broccoli, or 1 pound (455 g) frozen broccoli**

**¼ cup (½ stick/55 g) unsalted butter**

**2 tablespoons all-purpose flour**

**1 cup (240 ml) milk, whole or 2%**

**½ cup (115 g) grated cheddar cheese, mild, medium or sharp**

**Pinch of salt**

**Paprika**

Wash the broccoli and cut into florets. In an 8-quart (7.5 L) pot, bring 4 quarts (3.8 L) water to a boil over high heat. Once boiling, add the broccoli, and cook for 3 minutes. Drain and set the broccoli aside.

Make the cheese sauce: In a 2-quart (2 L) saucepan, melt the butter over low heat. Be very careful not to burn the butter.

Once the butter is melted, stir in the flour, then slowly pour in the milk. Stir the mixture constantly until it's smooth and thickened. Add the cheese and salt, and stir until melted and smooth.

Pour the cheese sauce over the broccoli and garnish with paprika. Serve immediately.

# Slaw

SERVES: 8 TO 10

I LOVE A GOOD SLAW. THESE DAYS, YOU SEE COLESLAW WITH BARBECUE, ON SANDWICHES, AND THINGS LIKE THAT. I like my coleslaw with any bird, like a good fried or baked chicken. The key to coleslaw is using just the right amount of mayonnaise. Too much, and you've got a mushy side; too little, and you've got a dry bowl of vegetables. How you slice your vegetables will determine just how the mayonnaise holds. Serve this dish with my fried chicken (page 149), baked chicken (page 141), or fried fish (page 63).

**1 large head green or red cabbage, shredded**

**1 carrot, grated**

**1 (145 g) bell pepper, sliced**

**1 cup (160 g) peeled and diced red apple**

**1 tablespoon sugar**

**2½ tablespoons cider vinegar**

**1 teaspoon celery salt, plus more to taste**

**1 teaspoon fresh lemon juice (from 1 lemon), or 1 teaspoon lemon juice**

**1 cup (240 ml) mayonnaise, plus more if needed**

Using a large spoon or salad hands, mix the cabbage, carrot, bell pepper, apple, sugar, vinegar, celery salt, lemon juice, and mayonnaise together in a large mixing bowl. If the salad is too dry, add more mayonnaise. Be careful, though—adding too much mayonnaise can make the salad too soggy.

# Corn Fritters

SERVES: 4 TO 6

CORN FRITTERS ARE MADE JUST LIKE PANCAKES. The key to perfectly golden fritters is flipping them just once, which means knowing your griddle well enough to know when the underside of the fritter is fully cooked. Usually, you want to *just* smell the scent of the creamed corn. Once both sides are browned, they should be eaten immediately. Before I serve them, I like to top mine with just a sliver of butter, but you can add your own twist, like honey, syrup, or jelly.

**1 (16-ounce/455 g) can creamed corn, undrained**

**¼ cup (½ stick/55 g) unsalted butter, melted**

**½ cup (65 g) self-rising flour, preferably White Lily**

**1 teaspoon sugar**

**2 large eggs, beaten**

Preheat an electric pancake griddle to 375°F (190°C).

In a medium mixing bowl, combine the creamed corn, melted butter, flour, sugar, and eggs. Mix together until combined.

Spoon the mixture out onto the griddle, shaping the mixture into mini pancakes. Cook the fritters until browned on one side, about 3 minutes; turn just once, and allow the fritter to brown on the other side. Serve immediately.

# Corn Pudding

SERVES: 4 TO 6

I LEARNED TO MAKE SOME OF MY FAVORITE DISHES AT THE DODGE HOME, INCLUDING THIS CORN PUDDING. Creamed corn is a bit sweet, so this dish goes well with savory meat dishes, like pork or chicken.

**1 (16-ounce/455 g) can creamed corn, undrained**

**2 tablespoons all-purpose flour**

**½ cup (1 stick/115 g) unsalted butter, at room temperature**

**2 tablespoons sugar**

**1 teaspoon salt**

**3 large eggs, beaten**

Preheat the oven to 350°F (170°C). Grease a 9 by 13-inch (23 by 33 cm) baking dish.

In a large mixing bowl, mix together the creamed corn, flour, butter, sugar, salt, and eggs.

Pour the mixture into the prepared baking dish. Bake the pudding for 30 to 35 minutes. The corn pudding consistency should not be soupy or hard. Remove when the pudding ingredients have combined and the top of the pudding is golden brown.

*"Good cooks don't measure. They use the imagination of the brain, and the heart. If you put in your heart, it will always turn out good!"*

# Creamed Onion Casserole

SERVES: 10 TO 12

MY CREAMED ONION CASSEROLE GETS ITS FLAVOR FROM THE LIGHT SWEETNESS IN PEARL ONIONS AND THE PEPPERY TASTE OF PAPRIKA, AND IS TOPPED OFF BY THE CRUNCH OF BREAD-CRUMBS. Like most of my casserole sauces, you want to be careful not to make the sauce too thin or too thick. And like most of my recipes, if it's too thick, add a little more milk, and if it's too thin, take a little out with a small spoon. Pay attention to stirring the sauce so it comes out nice and smooth.

**20 pearl onions**

**½ stick/55 g) unsalted butter**

**2 tablespoons all-purpose flour**

**1½ cups (360 ml) milk, whole or 2%**

**½ teaspoon Nature's Seasons, plus more to taste**

**¼ to ½ cup (30 to 55 g) grated cheddar cheese**

**¼ cup (25 g) breadcrumbs**

**Paprika (optional)**

Preheat the oven to 350°F (170°C).

Remove the skins from the pearl onions, similar to how you would peel regular onions. Fill a 4-quart (3.8 L) pot with 2 quarts (1.9 L) of cold water. Wash the onions and place them in the pot of cold water. Bring to a boil and cook for 2 minutes. Drain and place the cooked onions in an ungreased 9 by 13-inch (23 by 33 cm) baking dish and set aside.

In a 2-quart (2 L) saucepan, melt the butter over medium heat. Using a wooden spoon, stir in the flour. Add the milk and cook, stirring constantly, until the sauce thickens. Season with Nature's Seasons to taste.

Pour the sauce over the pearl onions. Sprinkle with the cheese, breadcrumbs, and paprika to taste. Bake for 15 to 20 minutes, until the casserole is bubbling and the edges are lightly browned.

# Eggplant Casserole

SERVES: 6 TO 10

ON EDISTO, WE GROW EGGPLANTS, SWEET POTATOES, AND EVERY OTHER VEGETABLE UNDER THE SUN. I like to get my eggplants fresh from my garden right here on the island, but you can get your eggplants wherever they're available. Just be sure that they are firm, but not hard as a rock. In this casserole, I mix and top my eggplant with shredded sharp cheddar cheese, but shredded mozzarella works great too.



**4 small eggplants**

**2 teaspoons Nature's Seasons**

**¼ cup (½ stick/55 g) unsalted butter, at room temperature**

**⅓ cup (35 g) breadcrumbs**

**2 large eggs, lightly beaten**

**⅓ cup (40 g) shredded cheddar cheese, plus ¼ cup (30 g) for the top of casserole**

**4 ounces (112 g) cream cheese**

Preheat the oven to 350°F (170°C). Lightly grease a 9 by 13-inch (22 by 33 cm) casserole dish.

Peel and chop the eggplants. In a large, heavy-bottomed pot, add enough tepid water to cover the eggplants. Season the water with the Nature's Seasons. Cook the eggplants over medium-high heat for 6 to 8 minutes, until tender. Thoroughly drain the eggplants and pat the pieces dry.

In a large mixing bowl, combine the butter, breadcrumbs, eggs, ⅓ cup (40 g) of the cheddar cheese, the cream cheese, and the cooked eggplant. Using a wooden spoon, mix the ingredients together.

Pour the mixture into the prepared casserole dish. Sprinkle the top of the casserole with the remaining cheese. Bake the casserole until golden brown, 35 to 40 minutes.

# Mashed Potatoes

SERVES: 6 TO 8

A LOT OF MASHED POTATOES TAKE A LITTLE BIT OF ELBOW GREASE, BUT IN MY RECIPE, I PUT THE ELECTRIC MIXER TO USE INSTEAD. I like to keep things simple. Just a bit of butter, cream, and salt makes this a lovely Thanksgiving dish. For a real dinner-table showstopper? You can make my chicken gravy (page 144) to serve with the potatoes.

**6 medium white potatoes (a little over 2 pounds/1 kg), rinsed, peeled, and quartered**

**½ stick (55 g) unsalted butter**

**Salt, to taste**

**⅓ cup (75 ml) whole milk or cream**

Rinse, peel, and quarter the potatoes.

In an 8-quart (7.5 L) pot, bring 4 quarts (3.8 L) water to a boil over high heat. Once boiling, add the potatoes and boil for 8 to 10 minutes, until tender.

Drain, then place the potatoes in a mixing bowl. Add the butter, salt, and milk. Mix together with an electric mixer until smooth. Serve alongside or with gravy.

# Hash Brown Potatoes (Home Fries)

SERVES: 6 TO 8

I LOVE COOKING POTATOES BECAUSE IT USUALLY JUST TAKES A FEW INGREDIENTS TO TURN THEM INTO SOMETHING YOU JUST CAN'T RESIST. These hash brown potatoes are easy to make, and the scallions add a bright, fresh flavor to the dish.

**8 yellow or white potatoes (a little over 2 pounds/910 g), diced**

**¾ cup (1½ sticks/170 g) unsalted butter**

**2 scallions (30 g), chopped**

**Salt to taste**

In a 4-quart (3.8 L) saucepan, bring 2 quarts (475 ml) water to a boil over high heat. Add the potatoes and boil for 3 to 4 minutes, until tender. Drain well.

In a 12-inch (30.5 cm) cast-iron skillet, melt the butter over low heat, taking care not to burn. Add the scallions and the potatoes to the skillet. Salt the potatoes according to taste. Cook over medium heat until golden brown.

When the potatoes are browned on the bottom, turn them with a spatula and brown the other side.

# Mushroom Fritters

SERVES: 6 TO 8

THE SLIGHTLY SWEET AND SAVORY ESSENCE OF MUSHROOMS SHINES IN THESE FRITTERS, EVEN WITH THE CRUNCHY, BROWNED SIDES. The eggs and flour help to bind the mushrooms and roux together, and the breadcrumbs add a flaky texture. These are good little snacks, especially when you have guests or people from the community coming over. Like my daughters Marvette Meggett and Mildred "Millie" Heyward say, "Mom feeds everybody in the community, cats, every creeping crawling thing. Everybody."

FOR THE MUSHROOMS:

**½ cup (120 ml) vegetable oil, divided**

**¼ cup (½ stick/55 g) unsalted butter, divided**

**16 ounces (455 g) mushrooms, cleaned and cut into small pieces**

**1½ teaspoons curry powder**

**Pinch of salt**

FOR THE CREAM SAUCE:

**1 sleeve (40) saltine crackers**

**2 large eggs**

**5 tablespoons (75 ml) milk, whole or 2%**

**½ cup (65 g) all-purpose flour**

Make the mushrooms: In a 12-inch (30 cm) skillet, heat ¼ cup (60 ml) oil and 2 tablespoons butter over medium heat. Once hot, add the mushrooms, curry powder, and a pinch of salt.

Heat over medium heat, stirring to ensure the mushrooms are coated with curry powder. Sauté for about 5 minutes, or until the mushrooms begin to produce liquid. Set aside and allow to cool for about 10 minutes.

While the mushrooms are cooling, make the cream sauce: Using a rolling pin, crumble the saltine crackers into breadcrumbs. Set aside.

In a large bowl, add the eggs and milk. Whisk until combined. Add the flour and whisk again. The mixture should be fairly thick. Add the cooled mushrooms to the bowl and, using a wooden spoon, fold the mushrooms into the sauce. Once combined, add the crushed saltine crackers and stir to combine. The mixture should be thick, but not dry. If it's too doughy, add more milk by the tablespoon.

Wipe the old oil and butter from the skillet and add the remaining oil and butter. Heat over medium-high heat. Using your hands, scoop out the mushroom mixture and make small patties. The patties should be thick rounds—about the size of the palm of your hand, and roughly 1½ inches (4 cm) thick. Brown the patties for 4 to 5 minutes on each side.

# New Potato Casserole

SERVES: 6 TO 8

I LEARNED HOW TO MAKE NEW POTATO CASSEROLE WHEN I WAS WORKING AT THE DODGE HOUSE. I enjoyed making the casserole because there was this delicious sauce that stays with you, but guests could still taste the texture of the potatoes. This beautiful dish is wonderful for holidays or special events, and I suggest serving it with any bird, beef, or pork entrée.

**10 new potatoes (a little over 1¼ pounds/570 g), white or red, unpeeled**

**1 tablespoon salt, plus more to taste**

**½ stick (55 g) unsalted butter**

**2 tablespoons all-purpose flour**

**1⅓ cups (315 ml) milk, whole or 2%**

**⅓ cup (75 ml) half-and-half**

**1 teaspoon chopped fresh parsley, plus more for garnish**

**1 teaspoon chopped fresh chives, plus more for garnish**

**Paprika, for garnish**

Preheat the oven to 350°F (170°C). Grease a 9 by 13-inch (23 by 33 cm) baking dish.

Wash the potatoes. Remove any eyes from the potatoes. Cut the larger potatoes in half; do not cut up the smaller potatoes.

In a 4-quart (3.8 L) pot, combine 2 quarts (2 L) water and 1 tablespoon salt. Bring to a boil. Add the potatoes, reduce the heat to medium-high, and cook until the potatoes are tender, 10 to 12 minutes.

Once the potatoes are cooked, drain and place them in the prepared baking dish; set aside.

In a medium skillet, melt the butter over low heat. Stir in the flour until it's absorbed into the melted butter.

Slowly add the milk and half-and-half, making a sauce. Bring this sauce to a boil over high heat, continuing to stir until mixed well. Remove from the heat.

Add the parsley, chives, and a pinch of salt to the sauce. Add more salt if needed.

Pour the sauce over the potatoes in the baking dish and bake for 20 minutes. Garnish with more parsley and chives, and paprika. Serve immediately.

# Squash Casserole

SERVES: 10 TO 12

SQUASH CASSEROLE USES SOME OF MY FAVORITE VEGETABLES—SQUASH AND ZUCCHINI. I like to use cream cheese in my casserole because it helps to bring very different ingredients together, and it adds richness and creaminess to otherwise gritty veggies.

**3 medium yellow squash, thinly sliced into rounds about ⅛ inch (3 mm) thick**

**3 medium zucchini, thinly sliced into rounds about ⅛ inch (3 mm) thick**

**1 (8-ounce/225 g) pack cream cheese, at room temperature**

**¼ cup (½ stick/55 g) unsalted butter, at room temperature**

**1 cup (110 g) grated medium or sharp cheddar cheese**

**1 large egg, lightly beaten**

**2 teaspoons Nature's Seasons, plus more to taste**

Preheat the oven to 350°F (170°C).

Bring a large pot of water to a boil. Add the squash and zucchini, bring back to a boil, and cook until tender, about 10 minutes. Drain very well in a colander, making sure to shake all the excess water out.

In a large mixing bowl, combine the cream cheese, butter, ½ cup (55 g) of the cheddar cheese, and the egg, then stir in the squash. Mix well. Add Nature's Seasons—more if needed—and stir again.

Pour the squash mixture into an ungreased 9 by 13-inch (23 by 33 cm) baking dish. Sprinkle the top of the casserole with the remaining cheddar cheese.

Bake the casserole for 35 to 40 minutes, until golden brown on top. Let cool for a few minutes before serving.

# Stuffed Bell Peppers

SERVES: 8

STUFFED BELL PEPPERS WERE ANOTHER HIT DISH AT THE DODGE HOUSE, AND MANY OTHER HOMES I COOKED IN ON EDISTO. These bell peppers are like hamburgers without the bread, and with a lot more flavor. I love stuffing bell peppers because you don't have to waste much, and there are lots of opportunities for creativity. Just one of these hefty, meaty stuffed peppers can be a meal in itself, and they're real pretty to look at, too.

**8 bell peppers, whole; plus ½ bell pepper, grated**

**1½ pounds (680 g) ground beef**

**1 medium onion, grated**

**2 tablespoons Worcestershire sauce**

**1 teaspoon seasoning salt, preferably Gold Medal, plus more to taste**

**2 large eggs, beaten**

**1 teaspoon fresh lemon juice**

**⅓ cup (35 g) breadcrumbs**

**1 tomato, chopped**

**Grated cheddar or mozzarella cheese, for garnish (optional)**

Preheat the oven to 350°F (170°C).

Wash the bell peppers. Cut off the tops of all the peppers and scoop out the insides. Wash the peppers again, removing all the seeds.

Place the peppers in cold water to keep crisp, bottom side down. Set aside.

In a mixing bowl, mix together the ground beef, onion, grated bell pepper, Worcestershire sauce, seasoning salt, eggs, lemon juice, breadcrumbs, and tomato.

In a large skillet, cook this mixture on medium heat for 5 to 6 minutes, until the beef is thoroughly cooked and browned. Taste and add more seasoning salt if needed. Do not overcook—veggies should still have a bit of their form and shouldn't be too softened.

Remove the meat mixture from the stove. Drain off any excess grease from the mixture.

Pour ¼ cup (60 ml) water into a 9 by 13-inch (23 by 33 cm) baking dish. Stuff each bell pepper with the meat mixture and place in the baking dish. The water will keep the bottom of the peppers from burning.

Bake the stuffed peppers for 20 to 25 minutes, until the peppers are tender. Remove the dish from the oven and sprinkle cheese on the top of the peppers, if using. Return the baking dish to the oven and continue to bake for 5 to 10 minutes, until golden brown on top.

# Stuffed Yellow Squash and Zucchini

SERVES: 7

BACK IN MY DAY, WE REALLY LIKED TO FILL VEGETABLES WITH ALL SORTS OF NEW FOODS AND FLAVORS. I loved making stuffed zucchini and squash because you could use all of the vegetable parts and create a tasty side that everyone would enjoy, even the children. The bacon flavor works well with the nutty flavor of the squash, and it gives the zucchini, which has a much more subtle taste, some added flavor and punch. The breadcrumb topping is essential—it adds a little crunch to an otherwise tender, buttery dish. This savory side goes well with my baked chicken (page 141).

**5 yellow squash**

**2 zucchini**

**4 slices bacon, fried until crisp, chopped**

**¼ cup (½ stick/55 g) unsalted butter, at room temperature**

**½ cup (50 g) breadcrumbs, plus more for topping**

**½ scallion, thinly sliced**

**Seasoning salt**

Preheat the oven to 350°F (170°C).

In a 12-quart (11.4 L) pot, bring 8 quarts (7.5 L) dry water to a boil over high heat. (When I say "dry water," that means just plain water—no salt added.) Add the whole yellow squash and zucchini to the pot and boil for 4 minutes.

After the vegetables are cooked, drain the hot water and replace it with cold water to cool the squash. When the squash and zucchini are cool enough to handle, cut each one in half lengthwise, and cut off the narrow necks of the yellow squash. Chop the necks into pieces. Place the necks in a bowl and set aside.

Remove the insides of each squash and zucchini half and add them to the necks.

Place the halves in a 9 by 13-inch (23 by 33 cm) baking dish.

To the necks and insides, add the bacon, butter, breadcrumbs, scallion, and seasoning salt to taste. Mix the ingredients together thoroughly. Use this mixture to fill each yellow squash and zucchini cavity.

Sprinkle the top of each stuffed squash and zucchini with breadcrumbs. Pour ¼ cup (60 ml) tepid water into the bottom of the baking dish to prevent the squash from burning.

Bake the stuffed squash for 20 to 25 minutes, until the squash is cooked and slightly golden.

# Pimento Cheese

SERVES: AT LEAST 10

KNOWN AS THE "CAVIAR" OR THE "PÂTÉ" OF THE SOUTH, PIMENTO CHEESE IS SOMETHING EVERYONE IN THE DEEP SOUTH, AND ESPECIALLY IN THE CAROLINAS, HAS AN OPINION ABOUT. Pimento cheese should have the consistency of a relish or a toast spread—not too thick, not too thin. I love to eat my pimento cheese with crackers, but you can add pimento cheese to sandwiches, turn it into a sauce for poultry, and even serve it as a dip for vegetables. The pimentos pack a punch, now, but it's a hit you'll want to take.

**½ (8-ounce/225 g) block mild cheddar cheese, grated**

**½ (8-ounce/225 g) block sharp cheddar cheese, grated**

**2 (4-ounce/113 g) jars diced pimentos, undrained**

**1 tablespoon ketchup**

**1½ teaspoons sugar**

**1 tablespoon Worcestershire sauce**

**1 tablespoon hot sauce, plus more to taste**

**¾ cup (180 ml) Hellmann's mayonnaise, plus more if needed**

In a large mixing bowl, combine all the ingredients and mix with a large spoon. The mixture should be light, similar to a toast spread. If it's too thick, add more mayonnaise, 2 table-spoons at a time. Once the cheese mixture is combined, chill overnight in the fridge.

# Fried Green Tomatoes

SERVES: 6 TO 8

GREEN TOMATOES CAN BE EITHER HEIRLOOM TOMATOES, OR RED TOMATOES THAT AREN'T YET RIPE. Both are absolutely delicious when seasoned and fried. If you pick a green tomato and hide it in a cool, dark place, it stops the ripening. Put them on a newspaper under your bed or in a dark closet, and they will keep for weeks. When you're ready, move them to the kitchen windowsill or the sun porch's table. It is better to sit the tomato face-up while storing. People don't like to sleep facedown, and tomatoes don't either. You may serve these with my pink sauce (page 277).

**3 green tomatoes**

**½ cup (60 g) white cornmeal**

**⅓ cup (75 ml) vegetable oil**

**1½ teaspoons salt**

Cut the tops off the tomatoes. Slice each tomato into ½- to 1-inch (12 mm to 2.5 cm) rounds.

Place the tomato slices in a large bowl. Add the white cornmeal to the bowl, and coat each slice separately. Use your hands to cover the tomatoes in cornmeal so both sides are coated. Lay the coated tomatoes in a single layer on a plate.

In a large skillet, heat the oil on medium-high heat. Place the tomatoes in the hot oil one at a time until the skillet is full. Cook the tomatoes for 4 to 5 minutes on each side. They should be golden brown on both sides. Once browned, remove and place on a paper towel to absorb excess oil. Repeat with the remaining tomatoes. Place on a platter and serve hot.

# Tomato Casserole

SERVES: 10 TO 12

THE TOMATOES ON EDISTO ARE SOMETHING ELSE. They're big, they're juicy, and they're just not like the tomatoes you get in the big city these days. I love growing tomatoes in my garden, so when summer comes and it's time to pick them, I get excited about how many different ways I can use them in my cooking, like in this casserole. A little sweet and tangy, tomato casserole is a bowl of comfort during our warm South Carolinian months. Because the consistency is closer to a soup, I suggest serving it with something like fried fish (page 63), fried chicken (page 149), or fried turkey wings (page 152).

**8 slices white bread**

**7 large tomatoes**

**¼ cup (½ stick/55 g) unsalted butter**

**2½ tablespoons sugar**

**1½ tablespoons Nature's Seasons, plus more to taste**

Preheat your oven's broiler to 500°F (260°C) or its highest setting. On your oven's highest rack, broil all the bread slices for 2 to 3 minutes, until golden and crisp but not burned. Flip all the slices over and broil for another 2 to 3 minutes. Turn the broiler off and allow the bread to crisp in the oven for 15 minutes. Remove the bread from the oven and set aside.

Preheat the oven to 350°F (170°C).

Wash, peel, and quarter the tomatoes.

In a large, heavy-bottomed pot, cook down the tomatoes for 30 to 40 minutes over medium heat. The tomatoes should be combined and have the texture of a sauce.

When the tomato mixture has been cooked down, add the butter and allow it to melt into the cooked tomatoes. Add the sugar to cut the acid of the tomatoes, and season with Nature's Seasons.

Cut off the crusts from all but two slices of the toast. Cut the toast into small squares. Line the bottom of a 9 by 13-inch (23 by 33 cm) baking dish with half of the toasted squares. Grate the two remaining pieces of toast and set the breadcrumbs aside.

Carefully spoon half of the tomato mixture into the casserole dish on top of the toast, until the toast is covered. Add the remaining toast squares to the dish and cover again with the remaining tomato mixture. Sprinkle the top of the tomato casserole with the breadcrumbs. Bake for 30 to 35 minutes, until bubbly.

# Fried Zucchini

SERVES: 6 TO 8

I THINK OF FRIED ZUCCHINI AS VEGETABLE CHIPS. I slice my zucchini thin (but not too thin, as you'll want to taste the vegetables, not just the breading), and season them with some salt before dipping them in a light batter and dropping them in the frying oil. You should fry these until they're golden brown and serve them immediately. When you are going to fry anything, the oil must be hot enough so whatever you put in there does not absorb the oil, but not so hot that it smokes.

**3 medium zucchini, sliced into rounds about ⅛ inch (3 mm) thick**

**1 tablespoon salt**

**1 large egg**

**⅓ cup (75 ml) milk, whole or 2%**

**½ cup (65 g) self-rising flour**

**2½ cups (600 ml) vegetable oil**

Sprinkle the salt evenly onto the zucchini (use more salt if you like your veggies a bit more salty). Set the salted zucchini aside.

In a large mixing bowl, combine the egg and milk. Add the zucchini slices, and make sure that every slice is coated in liquid.

Place the flour in a large paper bag (a grocery bag will do). Remove the zucchini slices from the wet mixture and add them to the bag with flour. Close the top of the bag and shake, shake, shake! Toss the ingredients back and forth, enough to where all of the zucchini slices are coated in the flour.

In a 12-inch (30.5 cm) cast-iron skillet, heat the cooking oil to a high temperature. Drop each zucchini slice carefully into the hot oil, make sure there is enough oil so the zucchini slices will float; cook in batches. Brown the zucchini on both sides until crisp. This should take no more than 5 minutes total.

Line a plate with two paper towels, and place the zucchini on the paper towels to allow the oil to drain. Serve immediately.

# Collard Greens

SERVES: 8 TO 10

COLLARD GREENS HAVE A SPECIAL PLACE IN AFRICAN AMERICAN CULTURE. They're served at picnics, cookouts, dinners, and holidays. These dark green, bitter leaves turn into tender, juicy bites once they're slow-cooked with pepper, cider vinegar, sugar, seasoning, and that one magic ingredient: ham hock. The key to making really good collards is to keep them submerged in liquid so they don't dry out. There should always be at least a quart of liquid in the greens, and when you serve them, you want a bit of that savory broth on the serving spoon. Collard greens aren't like chicken—you can't overcook them. And you can eat collard greens with absolutely anything. You plant collard greens in August or September, so you can harvest and eat them for Thanksgiving.

I serve collard greens a lot, but I always make sure to cook them for New Year's Eve, following a tradition that goes all the way back to the middle of the nineteenth century. On New Year's Eve, my family eats hoppin' John for luck, and collard greens for wealth. This collard greens dish? This is the moneymaker dish right here.

**1 bunch collard greens (½ pound/225 g)**

**1 (14-ounce/400 g) smoked ham hock**

**2½ to 3 quarts (2.4 to 2.8 L) water**

**Crushed red pepper**

**1½ tablespoons cider vinegar**

**1 teaspoon sugar, or 2 packages sweetener**

**Nature's Seasons, to taste**

Wash the collard greens in cold water three or four times to remove any sand or dirt. Pat dry using a paper towel.

Strip the collard greens, removing the center stem. Cut the collard greens lengthwise into small, bite-sized pieces.

Wash the ham hock. In a large pot, combine the ham hock and water, and bring to a boil. Reduce the heat to medium, then add the greens, covering them in the water.

Add crushed red pepper to taste, the vinegar, sugar, and Nature's Seasons to taste. Increase the heat and bring back to a boil. Reduce the heat to medium and cook the greens for at least 2½ hours. After 2½ hours, taste the greens to test flavor and tenderness. Add more Nature's Seasons and cook longer, if necessary.

# Fruit Salad

MAKES: 1 LARGE SALAD

I USE SOME OF MY FAVORITE SUMMERTIME FRUIT TO MAKE THIS BEAUTIFUL FRUIT SALAD. A lot of this recipe is about designing the salad, so this dish is great to serve at big parties or celebrations.

**1 large watermelon (about 10 pounds/4.5 kg)**

**1 cantaloupe**

**2 kiwis**

**1 pound (455 g) grapes, red and/or green**

Cut the watermelon longways, take out insides, and place in a bowl. Scrape out the watermelon to the rind. Carve the watermelon rind around the edges (see photo).

Cut the cantaloupe, kiwis, and watermelon into bite-sized chunks. Add the cut watermelon, cantaloupe, kiwis, and grapes to the watermelon halves. Refrigerate to chill before serving.

# 3 | MEAT, POULTRY & WILD GAME

IF YOU'RE DRIVING DOWN AROUND ON EDISTO ISLAND, YOU MIGHT JUST RUN INTO A FAMILY. Not a family of people; a family of chickens, some turkeys, you might even see some geese.

Meat has a special place in Black culture, Gullah Geechee culture, and American culture. People have fried, baked, and broiled different types of birds around the globe, but the American versions come from indigenous, Black, and European traditions and culinary practices that can be seen in dishes like fish, turkey, baked chicken, and wings. Back in the old days, if we wanted chicken or turkey, we'd have to kill it, clean it, and, in some cases, preserve it to use later in the year. I'd season it and turn it into something new and tasty. Fried chicken (page 149) was always a favorite in my house, and us Gullah Geechee people can't get enough of chicken perloo (page 210).

In my community, we also can't get enough of good, well-seasoned meat. Many of the meals common in our culture now, like ham, barbecue, and pork chops, were developed by enslaved Africans during the country's earliest years, meeting the newfound tastes of white Americans. Though Native Americans were the original barbecuers in the United States, the American barbecue that we know today largely came from African American cooking. After some time, using rotating pits, making whole hog barbecue, and creating new rubs became what we know as American barbecue. Black folks became the barbecue experts. Europeans avoided the labor-heavy process, and enslaved African Americans learned and trained future generations to carry on these cooking traditions. Our ancestors were responsible for chopping the wood, starting the fires, killing the animals, processing them, digging trenches, filling those trenches with the coals, cooking the meat over hot coals, and seasoning and saucing the meat. They were also responsible for serving it to white guests and cleaning up afterward.

***"They used to have a bird they called the gannet. They were big white birds. My uncle used to go down there and shoot those birds. Mama used to cook it, and she used to cook it like she would cook chicken. Pre-fry it and stew it down. Put the onion on it and the green onion top. Girl, you talk about something that used to taste good!"***

Our love of good meat includes wild game, too. Edisto Island is filled with all kinds of wild animals. It was common for us to enjoy guinea fowl caught in a nearby field, ducks from the island's ponds and creeks, and even raccoon, known then as "coon"—which we used to eat with just a little salt. We would mix it up, too. Sometimes, Mama would use the insides of a quail and make a pâté. She would serve that pâté with the quail's head still attached. It may sound a little strange, but that's how we cooked and ate in those days.

Cooking wild game required skill—from hunting and catching the animals to learning how to cure and season them just right. This process wasn't easy. We'd have to clean the game, which meant taking off all the feathers, fur, or hides and cleaning out its insides. Preserving the wild game properly could mean curing or smoking the meat, which took a close eye and attention to detail. When my family would enjoy delicious, hearty meals that kept us full, often during those colder winter months, I remembered why the process was worth all the effort.

# Baked Chicken

SERVES: 4 TO 6

YOU CAN'T GO WRONG WITH A GOOD BAKED CHICKEN. I'd make this at home and at the Dodge House because it's simple to make, goes great with all sorts of vegetable and rice dishes, and the meat is tender and everyone will enjoy it. Check on the chicken regularly. If it browns too quickly, you'll have dried-out meat. As a thin sauce forms at the bottom of the dish, add a few spoons on top of the chicken about every 30 minutes. This will give you a chicken that's perfectly tender, and simply beautiful. I like cutting my chicken in half to bake it. Like most, I serve mine with rice, and on the serving plate I make sure to add some of the gravy from the bottom of the cooking dish.

**1 (6- to 7-pound/2.7 to 3.2 kg) whole chicken, cleaned and cut in half**

**1½ tablespoons seasoning salt, preferably Gold Medal, plus more to taste**

**2 tablespoons self-rising flour, preferably White Lily**

**½ onion, sliced**

Preheat the oven to 350°F (170°C).

Remove the backbone from the chicken. Season the chicken halves with the seasoning salt. Add more seasoning salt if desired.

Flour the chicken lightly, making sure that every part of the chicken is covered. Turn the chicken skin side up, and place it in a 9 by 13-inch (23 by 33 cm) baking dish. Spread the onion slices across the chicken, then pour 2 cups (480 ml) tepid water over the chicken.

Bake the chicken, uncovered, for 1½ hours, until brown and crispy, basting every 30 minutes during the cooking process by spooning the liquid from the bottom of the dish and over the top of the chicken.

Remove from the oven. There should be a thin, brothy sauce at the bottom of the dish, which you can serve with the chicken, with rice.

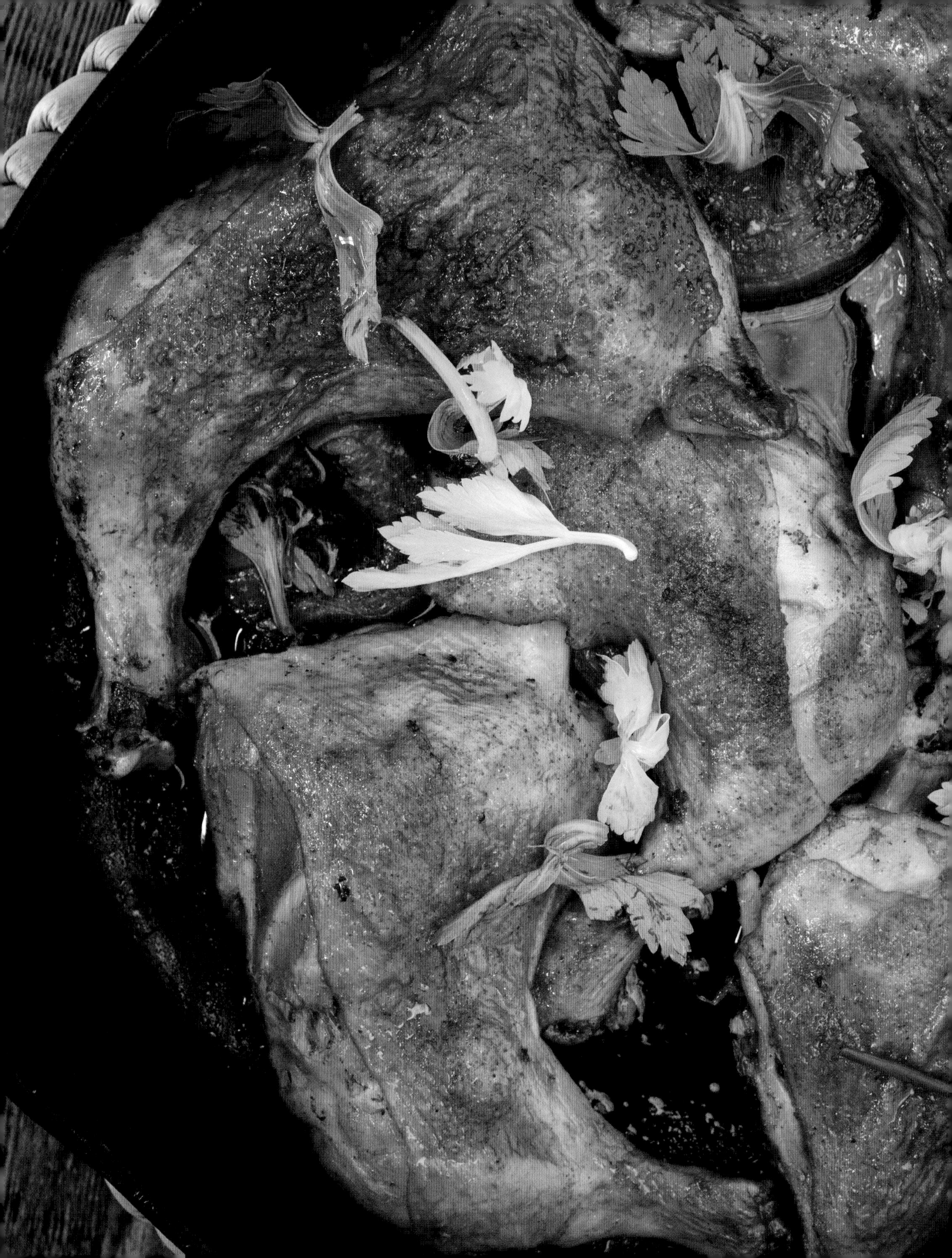

People of today, they don't wash the chicken. They just take it out the store, season, and cook it. Back in my time, you couldn't cook it like that—you had to wash it. You would have to take that fat off, take the hair, take the feather off. Then you would wash it, and wash it. My grandmother taught me to do that. Chicken is a nasty thing, now—underneath that skin, it's slimy.

Chicken of today is different than it was back then. Back then, everybody had their own chicken, so they didn't have to go to the store. If you wanted chicken, you'd take that chicken off the yard and fasten it up in another little coop, and let it sit in there for two, maybe three days. Then you'd kill this chicken. You'd chop the head off, then put the chicken in that hot water and get all the feather and things off there. Then you cut it up, clean it, season it, and you got your chicken ready to cook. But as for me? I washed it, no matter what.

Today, the world has learned more about how to safely handle meat and chicken. The Centers for Disease Control and Prevention (CDC) recommends not washing raw chicken. This may be different from my time, but I want everyone to be as safe as they can be in the kitchen, even when it looks a little different than my day.

# Chicken Gravy

SERVES: 8 TO 10

SOME GRAVIES CAN TAKE A WHILE TO MAKE, BUT WITH TEN CHILDREN, A HUSBAND, AND A BUSY JOB, I DIDN'T ALWAYS HAVE HOURS TO SPEND ON GRAVY MAKING. This gravy takes some time, sure, but you get a lot of good flavor much quicker than most recipes. I put gravy on just about everything, but you can start by adding yours to mashed potatoes (page 113).

**2 pounds (910 g) chicken livers, gizzards, and backs**

**1 onion, chopped**

**1 rib celery, chopped**

**¼ cup (½ stick/55 g) unsalted butter, melted**

**3 tablespoons all-purpose flour**

**Seasoning salt to taste**

**½ teaspoon Kitchen Bouquet**

In a large, heavy-bottomed pot, bring 4 quarts (3.8 L) water to a boil over high heat.

Add the chicken livers, gizzards, and backs to the water, along with the onion and celery, and boil until gizzards and backs are slightly tender, 40 to 45 minutes.

Remove the backs from the broth and discard. Cut up the livers and gizzards, then return them to the broth and set aside.

In a 12-inch (30.5 cm) cast-iron skillet, melt the butter. Add the flour to the butter, stirring constantly, until all the flour is absorbed. Slowly add 3 cups (720 ml) of the chicken broth and the livers and gizzards. Bring to a boil, stirring constantly. Cook for 5 minutes. Season the gravy with seasoning salt, adding more as needed. Add the Kitchen Bouquet for color.

# Creamed Chicken

SERVES: 8 TO 10

CREAMED CHICKEN IS ONE OF THE MEALS FROM MY DAY THAT YOU DON'T SEE A LOT ANYMORE, BUT YOU SHOULD. In those days, we needed meals that could sustain us. We all did laborious work, and these fast-food dinners they've got out here now just wouldn't cut it. This dish here has substance. The mushroom and herb sauce turns this simple cooked chicken breast into a hearty, flavorful dish. Serving it over grits, toast, or rice will have you full for the evening. If you'd like to prepare this dish as a casserole, see my tip below.

FOR THE CHICKEN:

**6 to 8 boneless, skinless chicken breasts**

**4 ribs celery, roughly chopped**

**2 scallions**

**Seasoning salt to taste**

FOR THE CREAM SAUCE:

**¼ cup (½ stick/55 g) unsalted butter**

**4 tablespoons (30 g) all-purpose flour**

**1 cup (240 ml) milk, whole or 2%, or chicken broth from cooked chicken**

**1½ cups (145 g) white mushrooms, plus more as desired, cleaned and chopped**

**1 tablespoon chopped fresh parsley**

**1 tablespoon chopped fresh chives**

Make the chicken: In a large, heavy-bottomed pot, bring 4 cups (960 ml) water to a boil over high heat. Once boiling, add the chicken breasts, celery, scallions, and seasoning salt. Cook until the chicken is cooked through, about 30 minutes. Be careful not to overcook. To see if the chicken is done, insert a knife in the thickest part of one breast. If it's still pink, continue to cook until you can see the cooked color of the meat all the way though the chicken.

Once the chicken is cooked, drain, reserving 1 cup (240 ml) of the broth with some celery and onion to use later for the sauce. Set the chicken aside, and allow the chicken to cool for 20 to 25 minutes.

Once the chicken has cooled, cut the chicken into small pieces. Set aside.

Make the cream sauce: In a 12-inch (30.5 cm) skillet, melt the butter over low heat. Once melted, add the flour and stir to combine. Stirring the mixture constantly, add the milk or the reserved chicken broth. After thoroughly mixing, bring this mixture to a boil and cook for 3 to 5 minutes, until thickened. Carefully add the cooked chicken without breaking up the pieces. Add the desired amount of chopped mushrooms, stir gently, and cook over medium heat for about 3 minutes. Remove from the heat and sprinkle with the parsley and chives.

**TIP: This may also be served as a casserole. If preparing this as a casserole, pour the chicken and cream sauce mixture into a greased 9 by 13-inch (23 by 33 cm) baking dish and sprinkle the top with parsley and breadcrumbs. Bake at 350°F (170°C) for 20 to 25 minutes, until bubbling.**

# Tomato Stuffed with Chicken or Turkey Salad

SERVES: 10

MY CHURCH COMMUNITY IS ONE OF THE MOST IMPORTANT PARTS OF MY LIFE. Through church, not only do I deepen my connection with God, I get to connect with my community. Like many churches in the South, we have spring and summer picnics to celebrate the warmer days, and catch up on the lives of friends and loved ones. One year, the church asked me to make a dish, and I just so happened to have some juicy tomatoes at home that an old friend brought me. I said to myself, "What if I stuffed these?" I cut out the center of the tomato and replaced it with some chicken salad I made the day before. It was a hit at the picnic, and I've made it ever since.

You can carve out the body of the tomato however you want, but whatever you do, don't waste it. My momma used to say, "Waste not, want not." If you core a tomato, and you're not going to use the inside at that time, save it and put it in a salad. Anything that is leftover, save it, 'cause you can always use it. If not today, you can use it tomorrow. I like to use my saved tomato for a side salad, a casserole, or a delicious sauce. We don't waste food here on Edisto Island, and I hope you won't either. For this recipe, you may use 2 cups (390 g) chopped cooked turkey instead of chicken.

**6 boneless, skinless chicken breasts**

**½ cup (30 g) sliced scallions**

**1 cup (100 g) chopped celery**

**3 hard-boiled eggs, chopped**

**1 tablespoon mustard**

**1 teaspoon celery salt**

**1 teaspoon poultry seasoning**

**2 cups (460 ml) Hellmann's mayonnaise, plus more if needed**

**10 large tomatoes**

Boil the chicken breasts and scallions in a pot of water until the chicken is cooked through, 25 to 30 minutes.

Remove the skin from the chickens, and let cool. When the chicken is completely cooled, cut it into small pieces and put in a large bowl.

Add the celery, hard-boiled eggs, mustard, celery salt, poultry seasoning, and mayonnaise and stir to combine. If the mixture is too dry, add more mayonnaise. Stir, taking care not to break up the chicken pieces.

Place the salad in the refrigerator to chill. (You may make the chicken salad a day ahead.) Cut the tops off of the tomatoes. Use a small paring knife to remove the inside of each tomato. A spoon may be helpful in scooping out the insides.

Once you've removed the insides of the tomatoes, fill the tomatoes with the chilled chicken salad. Be generous—it's called stuffed tomato for a reason!

# Fried Chicken

SERVES: 20 TO 30

IN THE SOUTH, AND HERE ON EDISTO ISLAND, WE LIKE OUR CHICKEN SIMPLE: GOLDEN BROWN, CRISPY, AND FRIED TO PERFECTION.

Similar to my fried shrimp, I prefer to coat my chicken with just enough breading to get a clean fry. Too much, and you'll have more fried flour than chicken. Cooking tools matter for this recipe. A cast-iron Dutch oven is preferable to a skillet; it allows the chicken to "float" in the oil and not stick as easily, while also browning it evenly. When the chicken starts floating to the top, you know it is almost ready—especially chicken and shrimp. If you don't get it right the first time, it's okay. You can always try again.

**Chicken pieces: 8 legs, 8 thighs, 8 wings, 4 whole breasts (10 pounds/4.6 kg total)**

**1½ tablespoons seasoning salt, plus more to taste**

**4 quarts (3.8 L) vegetable oil**

**4 cups (500 g) self-rising flour, preferably White Lily**

Peel back the chicken skin to reveal some unnecessary fat. Remove by scraping with a knife, and then put the skin back in place.

Season the chicken with seasoning salt.

Heat the oil in a cast-iron Dutch oven over high heat. Heat the oil to a high temperature, but be careful not to let it smoke.

Pour the flour into a large paper bag, such as a grocery bag. Add 6 to 8 chicken pieces to the bag at a time. Use one hand to close and grip the top of the bag, and one hand to support the bottom of the bag. Gently shake the bag from side to side, coating the chicken pieces with flour on all sides.

Fry these pieces, carefully placing them into the oil one at a time. Do not flour all the chicken pieces in advance. Flour them as they are fried.

Once the first batch of chicken is placed in the oil, reduce the heat to medium-high and cook the chicken on one side for about 20 minutes. Once golden brown, turn the chicken to brown on the other side, 8 to 10 minutes longer. The chicken will float when it is fully cooked. Regulate the temperature as needed. If the oil is not hot enough, the chicken will absorb the oil and become greasy.

When the first batch is finished, place the chicken on a paper towel–lined plate to drain. Repeat this process until done.

# Fried Turkey

SERVES: 8 TO 10

NOTHING GETS ME EXCITED AROUND THANKSGIVING QUITE LIKE MY FRIED TURKEY. The size of the turkey is up to you, but it is what you do with just four ingredients that matters. A turkey fryer is essential for this dish, and you want to make sure you pay attention to the oil temperature. This dish takes a little work and a little patience, but once you make it, you will never want to eat a baked turkey again!

**1 (16-pound/7.3 kg) whole turkey**

**Seasoning salt, preferably Gold Medal**

**Nature's Seasons, to taste**

**3 gallons (11.4 L) peanut oil**

Wash the turkey thoroughly, cleaning out the cavity, and pat dry with paper towels.

Rub the outside of the turkey with seasoning salt and Nature's Seasons.

Place the turkey in a baking dish. Cover with aluminum foil and place in the refrigerator for at least 24 hours, allowing it to absorb the flavors.

When ready to fry, go outdoors—for safety—and prepare the turkey fryer with the peanut oil according to the directions. Be sure to use a stable surface to prepare the fryer.

Heat the oil to 400°F (204°C). The oil should be tested for correct temperature so the turkey will not absorb the oil.

With great care, place the turkey on the rack and lower it into the oil.

Fry the turkey at 400°F (204°C) for 1 hour, or until golden brown, adjusting the heat as needed. Carefully lift it from the oil, transfer to a carving board, and serve.

# Fried Turkey Wings

SERVES: 4 TO 8

FRIED TURKEY WINGS ARE A GREAT OPTION FOR WEEKNIGHT DINNERS, AND CAN EVEN HAVE A PLACE ON THE HOLIDAY DINNER TABLE. A slower fry gets these tender and juicy, and you can enjoy these fresh or save them as leftovers for another meal.

**1 teaspoon Nature's Seasons, plus more to taste**

**1 teaspoon seasoning salt, plus more to taste**

**8 turkey wings, cleaned**

**5 cups (1.2 L) vegetable oil**

In a small bowl, combine the Nature's Seasons and seasoning salt.

Season each wing separately, coating the entire wing in the seasoning mixture. Set the seasoned wings aside.

In a large, heavy-bottomed pot, heat the oil over high heat. Once hot, reduce the heat to medium. Drop in the turkey wings and fry for 20 minutes, or until golden brown. Remove and place on a paper towel to absorb the oil. Place on a platter and serve hot or at room temperature.

# Chicken Liver with Onions

SERVES: 4 TO 6

THIS IS WHAT I CALL EASY COOKIN'. You sizzle some liver on both sides and make a quick gravy, and you've got yourself a good meal.

**4 to 6 pieces chicken liver**

**1½ tablespoons seasoning salt, preferably Gold Medal**

**¼ cup (60 ml) olive oil, bacon drippings, or vegetable oil**

**¼ pound (115 g) salt pork, sliced into 1-inch (2.5 cm) chunks**

**1 onion, sliced**

**1 bell pepper, sliced**

**2 heaping tablespoons all-purpose flour**

**About 3 cups (720 ml) water, plus more as needed**

**Cooked long-grain white rice, for serving**

Wash the liver, pat dry with paper towels, and season with seasoning salt.

In a 12-inch (30.5 cm) skillet, heat the oil over high heat. Once the oil is shimmering, reduce the heat to medium and add the liver. Cook the liver on one side until done, 5 to 7 minutes. Flip, and cook for about 5 more minutes, until it's a chocolate brown color on the outside and the center of the meat is no longer bloody. Once the liver is done, remove the liver from the skillet and place it on a paper towel. Set aside.

Pour off the grease from the skillet, and add the salt pork to the skillet. Fry the salt pork over medium heat for 5 to 7 minutes. Add the onion and bell pepper, and sauté with the salt pork until softened. Slowly add the flour, using a spoon to combine it with the sautéed pork and vegetables. Once all the flour is added, use a spoon to mix the ingredients together. Stir constantly while slowly adding water as needed and creating a gravy, cooking for about 10 minutes.

Turn the stove off. Put the liver back in the skillet. Put the gravy on top of the liver, and be careful not to let the gravy boil or cook. Serve with rice.

# Quail

SERVES: 4 OR 8

THESE DAYS, YOU DON'T HAVE TO GRAB A MUSKET TO GET A GOOD PIECE OF WILD GAME. Many butchers around the country offer wild game—usually specific to the region's specialties.

Like most wild game, quail are in season during the wintertime. Don't let that deter you, though—most wild game can be purchased, frozen, and preserved for a later time in the year. We'd usually eat these during December or January, and I'd freeze any extra quail for meals in the spring. Back then, they used to call the quail bird "partridge." And they were big. You eat quail, the little partridge, and you know, there's another water bird they used to catch called the marsh hen bird. You would have to catch them on high tide.

I found that many of the people I cooked for liked their quail rare, and with a little sherry. As for me? It has to be well-done. I will show you how to make both so you can decide just how you like your bird.

**8 quail (1 or 2 quail per person), cleaned**

**Seasoning salt**

**¼ cup (30 g) self-rising flour**

**4 slices bacon, cut in half**

**⅓ cup (75 ml) white cooking wine (optional)**

Wash the quail, pat dry with paper towels, and season with seasoning salt.

Lightly flour the birds and place them in a broiler-safe 9 by 13-inch (23 by 33 cm) glass baking dish, breast side up. Place one sliver of bacon on each breast.

**Broiled (Rare)**
Preheat your oven's broiler to 500°F (260°C), or its highest setting. On your oven's highest rack, broil the birds for 12 minutes.

Turn the broiler off. Add the wine to the dish and cover until ready to serve. Covering will cause the wine to steam into the quail. Serve 1 or 2 quail per person.

**Baked (Well-Done)**
Preheat the oven to 350°F (170°C).

Pour ½ to ¾ cup (120 to 180 ml) water into the baking dish with the quail, cover, and cook for at least 1 hour. Serve 1 or 2 quail per person.

# Backstrap of Venison

SERVES: 4 TO 6

WE DIDN'T KILL ANIMALS JUST FOR THE SAKE OF KILLING ON EDISTO—YOU TAKE ONLY DEER MEAT FOR YOUR FAMILY, AND TO LAST YOU THROUGH THE COLD MONTHS AND ANY UNEXPECTED TIMES. Those animals are precious, and it's important to respect the wildlife by not taking too much, or being greedy. The men would do the killing, and everyone would enjoy venison, or deer meat, during the winter months. Deer are all over Edisto (you've got to be really careful driving at night), so venison was easy to come by.

**Backstrap of venison**

**Seasoning salt**

**1 (16-ounce/473 ml) bottle Italian dressing**

Wash the venison, pat dry with paper towels, and season with seasoning salt as desired. Place in a 9 by 13-inch (23 by 33 cm) baking dish. Pour the dressing on top of the venison, and cover the dish. Put in the refrigerator to marinate overnight.

When ready to cook, prepare the grill. Grill the venison in the same way as steak or lamb chops. Turn the venison, browning both sides for 6 to 8 minutes. The center of the venison should be cooked, but slightly pink.

# Oven Bacon

SERVES: 6 TO 12

WHEN I WORKED AT THE DODGE HOUSE, THEY COULD TELL WHEN THE BACON WAS FRIED IN THE OVEN VERSUS WHEN IT WAS FRIED ON THE STOVE, BECAUSE IT LAYS IN THE OVEN, IT CURLS UP ON THE STOVE. Oven bacon has a more even crunch, and I still enjoy making my morning bacon just like this.

**12 slices thick-cut bacon**

Preheat your oven's broiler to 500°F (260°C), or its highest setting.

Arrange the bacon in a single layer in a rimmed baking pan and place it on the highest rack in your oven. Broil until browned on one side, about 2 minutes.

Turn the bacon and brown the other side. Watch the bacon closely. It will cook quickly, about 5 minutes total.

Remove from the oven and place the bacon on a paper towel to absorb the excess grease.

# Baked Pork Chops

SERVES: 6

A LOT OF TIMES AFTER LONG DAYS, I WOULD MAKE MY HUSBAND SOME BAKED PORK CHOPS. A lot of people dry out their pork chops, so you want to be careful and avoid heating your chops too fast or at too high a temperature. Serve the dish with rice, and be sure to get some of the meat's gravy on the serving plate too.

**6 bone-in pork chops**

**1½ tablespoons seasoning salt, preferably Gold Medal, plus more to taste**

**All-purpose flour, for dusting, plus 1 heaping tablespoon**

**2 cups (480 ml) vegetable oil**

**1 onion, sliced**

**½ bell pepper, sliced**

**1 teaspoon Kitchen Bouquet (optional)**

Preheat the oven to 350°F (170°C).

Wash the pork chops well and pat dry with paper towels. Sprinkle with seasoning salt, and dust both sides of each pork chop with flour.

In a 12-inch (30.5 cm) cast-iron skillet, brown the chops in the oil over medium-high heat for 5 to 6 minutes on each side.

Remove the pork chops from the skillet and place them in a deep 9 by 13-inch (23 by 33 cm) baking pan. Set aside.

Drain all but 2 tablespoons of the oil from the skillet. Sauté the onion and bell pepper in the remaining oil.

Add 1 heaping tablespoon flour to the skillet. Continue to stir while adding 2½ cups (600 ml) tepid water, and bring to a boil. Add the Kitchen Bouquet, if using, for color. Pour this gravy over the pork chops.

Cover the dish with foil and bake for 45 minutes.

# Barbecue Ribs and Sauce

SERVES: 6 TO 8

DURING AMERICA'S EARLIEST DAYS, WHITE AMERICANS DIDN'T WANT TO DO ALL OF THE WORK IT TAKES TO MAKE REALLY GOOD BARBECUE, SO BLACK FOLKS WERE THE PITMASTERS AND EXPERTS. The skill has been passed down through generations all over the country, and I learned how to make a mean rack of ribs from my own family. These ribs and sauce will have you licking your fingers after every bite, right up until you clean that bone right off.

**2 slabs baby back ribs**

**1 cup (100 g) chopped celery**

**1 large onion, chopped**

**1 bell pepper, chopped**

**1 to 2 tablespoons seasoning salt, to taste**

**3 tablespoons cider vinegar**

**1 cup (240 ml) ketchup**

**⅓ cup (145 g) packed brown sugar**

**1 lemon, sliced**

Preheat the oven to 350°F (170°C).

In a large, heavy-bottomed pot, precook the ribs with the celery, onion, bell pepper, seasoning salt, and vinegar in 2 quarts (1.9 L) of water for 35 to 45 minutes over medium heat, until the bones are just slightly peeking out, and the meat easily slides or peels off the bone. Remove the ribs from the stock and save 1½ cups (360 ml) of the liquid. Save the chopped celery, onion, and bell pepper. Set aside.

Place the ribs in a 9 by 13-inch (23 by 33 cm) baking pan, uncovered. Bake for 20 minutes. Remove from the oven and pour off the grease. (Leave the oven on.) With a fork, mash the celery, onion, and bell pepper.

In a medium saucepan, combine the ketchup, brown sugar, mashed vegetables, and reserved cooking liquid. Bring to a boil over high heat. Once boiling, pour over the cooked ribs. Place the lemon slices on top of the ribs. Cover. Return the ribs to the oven and bake for 25 to 30 minutes.

# Chuck Roast

SERVES: 6 TO 8

A GOOD CHUCK ROAST REQUIRES PATIENCE. This is a great dish to start in late afternoon or early evening when you're cleaning the house or doing at-home activities with your family, because it takes at least two and a half hours to bake. Just before it's ready, you can make some potatoes and boiled carrots to serve with the dish at dinnertime.

**2½ to 3 pounds (1.2 to 1.4 kg) chuck roast**

**Seasoning salt**

**1½ tablespoons all-purpose flour**

**1 large white or yellow onion, sliced**

**1 bell pepper, sliced**

**1 rib celery, chopped**

Preheat the oven to 350°F (170°C).

Wash the chuck roast, pat dry with paper towels, and season with seasoning salt. Dust both sides with the flour. Place the roast in an 11½ by 17-inch (29 by 43 cm) roasting pan. Add the onion, bell pepper, and celery. Add 3 to 3½ cups (720 to 840 ml) water and cover the pan with foil. Cook the roast in the oven for 2½ hours, or until tender.

If the roast is not tender after 2½ hours, continue cooking as needed, adding more water if necessary.

# Leftover Meat Casserole

SERVES: 6 TO 8

REMEMBER WHEN I SAID THERE'S NO WASTE? Here's a dish that shows those values. Use any type of leftover beef or meat to make this dish. The bouillon cube, which is used in a lot of West African dishes like jollof rice, soups, and stews, delivers an unmistakable salty and meaty flavor to this unassuming dish. When you're running on a short amount of time and just a few ingredients, this dish is great to have in your back pocket.

**2 cups (390 g) cooked beef, or any similar meat**

**1 cup (240 ml) milk, whole or 2%**

**½ cup (120 ml) half-and-half**

**2 (10¾-ounce/298 g) cans cream of mushroom soup**

**1 bouillon cube, chicken or beef, crumbled**

**Seasoning salt or Nature's Seasons to taste (less is required if using ham)**

**¼ teaspoon pepper**

**1 bay leaf, crumbled**

**¼ cup (30 g) grated onion**

**1 (16-ounce/455 g) package noodles of choice**

**⅓ cup (35 g) breadcrumbs**

**1 teaspoon paprika (optional)**

Preheat the oven to 350°F (170°C).

In a large bowl, combine the beef, milk, half-and-half, cream of mushroom soup, bouillon cube, seasoning salt, pepper, bay leaf, and onion.

Cook and drain the noodles according to the package directions.

Spread half of the cooked noodles in the bottom of an ungreased, rectangular, 9 by 13-inch (23 by 33 cm) casserole dish. Pour half of the meat mixture over the noodles. Repeat the layers. Top with the breadcrumbs and the paprika, if using. Bake for 20 minutes, or until bubbling. Serve over rice if desired.

# Meatloaf

SERVES: 10

MEATLOAF USES INEXPENSIVE INGREDIENTS AND CAN LAST FOR DAYS, EVEN FOR LARGE FAMILIES. I'd make this dish for my family when I wanted to cook something simple that would serve everybody. Because of the heartiness of this dish, we'd usually enjoy meatloaf in the fall or winter.

**2 pounds (910 g) ground beef**

**1 pound (455 g) lean bulk sausage, preferably Jimmy Dean**

**½ cup (50 g) breadcrumbs**

**1 large onion, grated**

**1 bell pepper, grated**

**2 tablespoons chopped parsley**

**2 large eggs**

**1½ teaspoons seasoning salt**

**¼ teaspoon pepper**

**1 tablespoon Worcestershire sauce**

**1 tomato, roughly chopped**

**Ketchup, to taste**

**Bell pepper slices (optional), for garnish**

Preheat the oven to 350°F (170°C).

In a large mixing bowl, combine all the ingredients, excluding the ketchup and water. Form the mixture into a loaf and place on a sheet of foil on the non-shiny side, then drizzle the top of the meatloaf with ketchup.

Tightly close the foil around the meatloaf. Place in a 5 by 9-inch (12 by 23 cm) loaf pan. Pour ¾ cup (180 ml) water around the foil package so the dish will not burn. Bake for 45 to 50 minutes, until well done. Garnish with bell peppers, if using.

# Pork Loin Roast

SERVES: 8 TO 10

THIS PORK LOIN ROAST CREATES ITS OWN GRAVY DURING THE COOKING PROCESS. The Kitchen Bouquet adds a bit more seasoning and gives color to the gravy, making it a deeper brown after it's done cooking.

**6 to 8 pounds (2.7 to 3.6 kg) pork loin roast**

**Seasoning salt**

**Self-rising flour, preferably White Lily**

**1 large onion, sliced**

**½ bell pepper, sliced**

**1 (0.7-ounce) package dry Italian dressing mix**

**1 teaspoon Kitchen Bouquet (optional)**

Preheat the oven to 350°F (170°C).

Rinse the pork loin and pat it dry with a paper towel. This will allow the seasoning to adhere. Sprinkle with seasoning salt to taste. Dust with flour.

Place the loin in a 10 by 14-inch (25 by 35.5 cm) roasting pan. Top with the onion and bell pepper. Sprinkle with the Italian dressing mix. Add 4 cups (960 ml) water and Kitchen Bouquet, if using, to the pan. Cover.

Bake for 2½ hours. Add more water during the cooking time, if needed.

# Salt Pork with Wild Cat Sauce

SERVES: 6 TO 8

YOU'VE NEVER HEARD OF THIS BEFORE, HAVE YOU? Don't be scared of the wild cat sauce, that's just what we call it on the island. My mama used to make this gravy for a neighborhood family when no meat was available. She "doubled up" the scallions from the family garden, and the gravy would still be so good that everyone wanted seconds. Give it a try—you'll want seconds too.

**½ pound (225 g) salt pork, sliced into 1-inch (2.5 cm) chunks**

**½ bunch scallions, chopped**

**2 tablespoons all-purpose flour**

**Seasoning salt**

Boil the salt pork in a medium pot of water for 6 to 8 minutes. Drain the water. Repeat.

Place the salt pork in a cast-iron skillet over medium heat and cover. The salt pork will "pop." Fry until crisp, 5 to 7 minutes.

Remove the meat from the skillet and pour off half of the grease. Sauté the scallions in the remaining grease until tender.

Add the flour and stir. Add seasoning salt to taste. Continue stirring while adding 2 cups (480 ml) water to the sauce. Bring to a boil. Add the cooked salt pork to the sauce and cook for 2 to 3 minutes longer.

# Saturday Poor Man Meal

SERVES: 6 TO 8

MY DAUGHTER ELIZABETH "DEEDEE" JONES REMEMBERS IT BEST: "ON SATURDAYS, WE'D HAVE PORK AND BEANS WITH RICE WITH SMOKED SAUSAGE. And butt's meat [salt pork]. Always a side of butt's meat."

Like my daughter, and the name, says, this was a Saturday meal. These ingredients were less expensive to get back in my day, yet when they come together over a bed of white rice, people all over smell it and come running to my house, asking for a plate. Sometimes, simple is better, and that's what you got with this poor man meal.

**2 (1-inch/2.5 cm) slices salt pork**

**1 large onion**

**2 links (8 ounces/225 g) smoked sausage**

**2 (11-ounce/312 g or 15-ounce/425 g) cans pork and beans, preferably Campbell's or Van Camp's**

Cut up the salt pork, wash it, pat dry with paper towels, and fry it in a large cast-iron skillet until crisp, 5 to 7 minutes.

Cut up the onion and add it to the salt pork. Cut up the sausage and add it to the pan. Cook over low heat for about 5 minutes. Add the pork and beans to the pan. Add 1 can of water to the pan. Let the meal simmer for at least 5 minutes, until the onion is tender.

*"You had a home-cooked meal every day. Even though my mom worked, when we got off the school bus, you could smell the food as soon as the bus put you off by the gate. You knew something good was waiting."* —MY DAUGHTER LAVERN MEGGETT

# Sausage and Gravy

SERVES: 4 TO 6

SAUSAGE AND GRAVY IS SOME GOOD EATIN'. Add more red pepper to kick up the spice in this dish, and serve it with homemade biscuits and grits any time of the day.

**3 slices bacon**

**¼ onion, chopped**

**2 tablespoons all-purpose flour**

**1½ to 2 cups (360 to 480 ml) water**

**⅓ ring smoked kielbasa, cut into pieces**

**Crushed red pepper**

**Seasoning salt**

**1 teaspoon Kitchen Bouquet (optional)**

Fry the bacon in a cast-iron skillet over medium-low heat until crisp.

Cut the bacon into pieces. Remove the bacon from the skillet and pour off half of the drippings from the skillet. Set the bacon aside.

Sauté the onion in the bacon grease in the skillet over medium heat until tender, for at least 7 minutes. Add the flour and mix with a fork. Gradually add the water, stirring with the fork, and bring to a boil.

Add the sausage to the gravy along with the bacon, and reduce the heat to low. Simmer long enough to cook the sausage, about 15 minutes.

Add crushed red pepper and seasoning salt to taste, and add the Kitchen Bouquet to deepen the gravy's brown color, if desired. Mix and cook for about 4 more minutes.

**TIP: A lot of people don't stir the gravy enough. To make smooth gravy, use a whisk the whole time instead of the fork. If you think the gravy is going to stiffen up on you or get lumpy, use the whisk. It will smooth the gravy out for you.**

# Meatballs

SERVES: 6 TO 8

WHEN I WAS LEARNING HOW TO COOK AS A TEENAGER, MEATBALLS WERE ONE OF THE FIRST DISHES I LEARNED HOW TO MAKE. I like to serve mine over rice. I don't like to cook my food way in advance and let it sit. That's not my style. I learned to cook and serve from the stove as soon as the food is done. When it's hot!

**1 (28-ounce/794 g) can diced or crushed tomatoes**

**1 (6-ounce/170 g) can tomato paste**

**1 large onion, chopped**

**1½ cups (150 g) chopped celery**

**1 large bell pepper, chopped**

**½ cup (110 g) packed brown sugar**

**1 teaspoon chopped fresh basil**

**1 teaspoon chopped fresh tarragon**

**Nature's Seasons, to taste**

**2 pounds (910 g) ground beef**

In a large pot, mix together 2½ cups (600 ml) water, the tomatoes, tomato paste, onion, celery, bell pepper, water, brown sugar, basil, tarragon, and Nature's Seasons, creating a sauce.

Cook for 1 to 2 hours over medium heat, until thick.

Preheat the oven to 350°F (170°C).

When the sauce is finished, form the beef into small balls and place them in an ungreased 9 by 13-inch (23 by 33 cm) baking dish.

Pour the sauce over the meatballs. Bake for 30 to 35 minutes, or until done.

9 CUPS
7 CUPS

*"Look out for people. Give and care. That's my motto. Food helps you do that."* —M.P.

# 4 | SOUPS & STEWS

I LEARNED HOW TO MAKE DIFFERENT TYPES OF SOUPS AND STEWS EARLY ON IN LIFE. Soups and stews didn't always require fresh ingredients; you could use seafood that had been saved from a previous season, vegetables reaching the end of their life cycle, and old stocks that had been frozen and preserved for a later date. When my uncle Henry would get shrimp from the creek in the springtime, Mama would dry it out, jar it, and preserve it for okra gumbo (page 184) in the wintertime. We made vegetable soup (page 187) using whichever crops we had growing in the garden. Okra soup (page 176), made with the okra we grew right in our garden, could soothe the soul, one cooked-down okra pod at a time.

I've made the soups and stews in this chapter throughout my life. All of them use seafood, meat, and crops available right here on Edisto Island, and available in grocery stores and markets around the country. Whether I was making a big ol' pot of Frogmore stew (page 180), which is really a boil, for a family cookout in the summertime, or a rich, slow-cooked beef stew at the Dodge House, cooking and serving them to people was always a pleasure. I wasn't just cooking for me, I was cooking for the folks I loved.

# Okra Soup

SERVES: 4 TO 6

THIS LOW-AND-SLOW-COOKED SOUP BREAKS DOWN THE OKRA AND SEASONINGS INTO A DELICIOUS POT OF GOODNESS. My son Christopher recalls, "When I had some of that okra soup? The plate was wiped clean!"

Okra can be a sensitive vegetable, so it's important to cook this soup at a very low temperature to avoid burning the okra. Shrimp is optional in this dish, but if you do use it, it should be cooked separately and added last.

**¼ pound (115 g) salt pork, cut into about 10 (1-inch/2.5 cm) chunks**

**4 pounds (1.8 kg) okra, cut into ½-inch (12 mm) pieces, or 2½ pounds (1.2 kg) frozen cut okra**

**1 onion (125 g), chopped**

**1 bell pepper (120 g), chopped**

**4 cups (960 ml) tepid water**

**1 tablespoon Nature's Seasons, plus more to taste**

**1 (6-ounce/170 g) can tomato paste**

**Seasoning salt, to taste**

**1 tablespoon sugar**

**½ pound (225 g) small shrimp, peeled and deveined (optional)**

**2 tablespoons unsalted butter, if using shrimp**

**Saltine crackers, to serve**

**Cooked long-grain white rice, to serve**

In a large, heavy-bottomed pot, fry 2 or 3 pieces of salt pork. Cook over medium-high heat for about 5 minutes, until browned and crisp.

In the same pot, add the remaining salt pork, the okra, onion, and bell pepper and sauté over medium heat in the salt pork fat for 12 to 15 minutes.

Add the water and Nature's Seasons and let it come to a boil. Reduce the heat to medium and let the mixture cook slowly for 1½ hours.

After 1½ hours, add the tomato paste, seasoning salt, and sugar and turn down the heat to low. Rinse out the tomato paste can and add 1 canful of water to the pot. Cook over low heat for 15 to 20 minutes. (If you don't turn down the heat to a low temperature and give it time to slowly simmer, it will burn.)

If you want to add shrimp, sauté the desired amount in the butter in a separate skillet until pink and add it to the okra soup just before serving; don't overcook the shrimp.

Serve over rice.

## *THE WOOD STOVE*

I was raised up at the woodstove. It had six burners, and had the oven just like a gas or electric stove. Then it had a warmer up to the top. If Mama cooked bread or sweet potato, she'd put it on that warmer. On the side, it had a big area where you had to put the water in there to get hot. And when it was time for you to take a bath, they had some big dippers. You'd have cold water in the tub, and you'd take the dippers and add hot water, and you'd have warm water to wash with.

Today, my children say, "Mommy, you don't need that woodstove." And I say, if you want to be friends with me now, don't mess with my woodstove.

# Oyster Stew

SERVES: 10 TO 12

REMEMBER WHEN I TOLD YOU THAT OYSTERS ARE BEST DURING THE MONTHS THAT HAVE THE LETTER *R*? Well, this oyster stew is a good example of why. Depending on the year, we would make oyster stew with fresh oysters caught in fall and winter, or we'd use frozen oysters. Now, fresh seafood is always preferable in any dish, but frozen oysters work just fine in this one.

Soups and stews were important during the winter months. I had a lot of mouths to feed, and a big pot of stew was one way I could feed my kids and use what we had on the land. *Don't ever put enough in the pot just for you. You never know who might come to see you, or be in need.* I suggest adding a dash of Worcestershire to each serving, and serving the stew with oyster crackers or crumbled saltines.

**¼ cup (½ stick/55 g) plus 2 tablespoons unsalted butter**

**1½ cups (150 g) diced celery**

**½ onion, diced**

**3 cups (720 ml) milk, whole or 2%**

**1 cup (240 ml) half-and-half**

**Seasoning salt, to taste**

**1 quart (905 g) shucked oysters**

**Worcestershire sauce, to taste**

**Oyster crackers or saltines, for serving**

In a large skillet, melt the ¼ cup (½ stick/55 g) butter over medium heat. Add the celery and onion and sauté until tender.

Pour the sautéed vegetables into the top of a double boiler. Add the milk and half-and-half, and bring water in the bottom of the double boiler to a boil.

Add seasoning salt to taste. Cook for 3 minutes.

Drain the oysters and place in a saucepan with the 2 tablespoons butter. Cook the oysters over medium heat until curled.

Transfer the oysters to the top of the double boiler with the milk mixture. Gently stir together. Serve with Worcestershire sauce and crackers.

# Frogmore Stew

SERVES: 8 TO 10

BACK IN THE DAYS WHEN EVERYONE USED TO COME OVER AND SPEND TIME TOGETHER AFTER A LONG WEEK OF WORK, WE'D ALL GATHER AROUND A BIG OL' POT OF FROGMORE STEW, OR, AS SOME LOCALS CALL IT, LOWCOUNTRY BOIL. No, frogs are not in this stew—don't worry! Instead, this soup includes Lowcountry staples—blue crab, shrimp, sausage, potatoes, and corn on the cob. Where does "Frogmore" come from, you ask? Well, I'll tell ya'. Frogmore is a very small, but mighty Gullah Geechee fishing community on St. Helena Island, just south of Edisto. There's a rich Black shrimping history on the island, and Frogmore stew is a meal that emerged from the plentiful seafood available in the South Carolina waters. We'd cook this dish outside, but these days, a large, heavy-bottomed pot on the stovetop does the trick. Here, you let the vegetables, aromatics, and seasoning do the talking, and the rest of the stew listens. You can serve this dish with my cocktail sauce (page 276), or just enjoy the stew's flavor. Get a big group of your closest family members together, and give this recipe a try on a late-summer night. It's the perfect time to eat with your hands and get a stomach full.

**1 dozen whole raw blue crabs, rinsed**

**2 gallons (7.6 L) cold water**

**2 medium onions, whole**

**¼ cup (48 g) Old Bay Seasoning or Maggi Seasoning**

**¼ cup (50 g) Gold Medal seasoning salt**

**2 pounds (910 g) smoked sausage links, cut into 3-inch (7.5 cm) chunks**

**6 ears corn, shucked and broken in half**

**12 red potatoes**

**6 pounds (2.7 kg) medium-sized shrimp, shells on**

**Cocktail sauce (page 276) to serve (optional)**

Remove the backs and the "dead man," the grayish crab gills (see my guide on page 59), from the crabs. Rinse the crabs and set aside.

On top of the stove, in a Dutch oven or other large heavy-bottomed pot, combine the water, onions, Old Bay, and Gold Medal. Boil for 10 minutes.

Add the sausage and crabs and cook for 10 minutes. Add the corn and cook for 5 more minutes.

Remove the eyes of the potatoes. Add the potatoes and shrimp to the pot and cook for 5 more minutes, or until the shrimp turns pink. Don't cook for too long, because you don't want the shrimp to dry out.

Once the stew is cooked, turn the stove off and drain the liquid from the stew using a strainer. Cover the top of a picnic table or long table with newspaper or paper bags. Pour the drained stew out from one end of the table to the other, and eat immediately with cocktail sauce, if desired.

JOURNAL REPORT | 5G TECHNOLOGY
5G TECHNOLOGY
A plan with release from civil liability for Purdue's owners.
What Is Happening in Other Markets

NEWSPAPER CARRIERS
WANTED!
$100 SIGNING BONUS
MYERS
$93
Weather
BASEBALL

# Okra Gumbo

SERVES: 8 TO 10

ENSLAVED AFRICANS BROUGHT MANY THINGS TO THE UNITED STATES, INCLUDING THEIR PRODUCE. Okra came along with the enslaved Africans, and it made American gumbos, stews, curries, and more possible. During the cold winter months, I make my okra gumbo on my woodstove. I know most people don't have those these days, but this gumbo works with whatever kind of stove you have. The sugar might seem strange to add to a vegetable recipe, but it helps to cut the acid from the tomatoes. You can serve this gumbo alone, or over a bed of white rice.

**¾ pound (340 g) salt pork, cut into 1-inch (2.5 cm) pieces**

**1 onion (125 g), chopped**

**1 bell pepper (120 g), chopped**

**1 (28-ounce/794 g) can crushed or diced tomatoes**

**1 (6-ounce/170 g) can tomato paste**

**3 pounds (1.4 kg) okra, cut into ½-inch (6 mm) pieces, or 2 pounds (910 g) frozen cut okra**

**Crushed red pepper**

**Gold Medal seasoning salt**

**1 tablespoon sugar, plus more to taste**

**1 (15¼-ounce/432 g) can corn, drained, or kernels cut from 2 ears fresh corn**

**1½ pounds (680 g) small shrimp, peeled and deveined (optional but recommended)**

In a large, heavy-bottomed pot, fry the salt pork over medium heat until crisp, 5 to 7 minutes. Add the onion and bell pepper and sauté together for 5 to 7 minutes, until translucent.

Add the tomatoes and tomato paste. Rinse out the tomato paste can and refill the can with water. Pour the water into the pot. Repeat this process two more times. Bring to a boil over high heat.

Turn down the heat to medium and cook for 25 to 30 minutes. If the mixture is too thick, add more water. Add the okra, crushed red pepper and seasoning salt to taste, and the sugar. Cook for 15 to 20 minutes.

Finally, add the corn and shrimp, stir, and cook the gumbo over low heat for about 10 more minutes. Serve with rice or eat plain.

## *OKRA AND GUMBO SHRIMP IN WINTER*

In the spring, my uncle would go in the creek and catch a lot of shrimp, and my grandmother would cook it. After she picked it, she would save the heads that would come off the shrimp. She spread the heads out on a cloth—a material they used to call "yellow husband." You spread it out on that, and let it dry. You put it out every day, take it in every afternoon, until it's dry, dry, dry. Mama would jar the shrimp, and she would take those heads, put them in a cheesecloth bag, and hang it up in the ceiling from the roof rafters. And then, when the winter come, that would be the winter food. You can't get any shrimp? She would just say, "Well, I'm gonna cook some okra gumbo, with shrimp."

And she had a roller—she would take that shrimp head, and roll it, and roll it . . . until it was like powder. Then she would put that in that okra gumbo, and you could smell it from the house to the gate.

And for the okra, she used to do the same—cut it up, put it on that sheet, and put it out every day in the sun until it's dry. Then we would get that okra and put it in a soak, in a big peach can, overnight. And when you wake up the next morning, that can would swell up to be a big pot full of okra.

They'd also do butter beans, peas, fish, oysters, tomatoes, and sweet corn the same way. I don't know how she did it, but she had a whole shelf of preserved ingredients. She'd clean the fish, take out the inside, hang it up, turn it into powder, and it would be just like it came out the creek.

They don't do that anymore.

# Vegetable Soup

SERVES: 10

I ALWAYS WANT YOU TO COOK WITH YOUR OWN TASTES IN MIND. This vegetable soup is a great chance to do just that. Though I list vegetables like bell peppers, tomatoes, butter beans, and carrots, you should feel free to use the vegetables you enjoy, and determine how many vegetables you need for the amount of soup you want. It's very easy to change the measurements here, and this soup works best when you use vegetables that are seasonal and are the best in whichever region you live. I suggest serving this soup with my homemade biscuits (page 214), saltine crackers, or toast.

**10 large tomatoes (1.8 kg), quartered or cut in half**

**1 large white or yellow onion (225 g), chopped**

**1 large bell pepper (165 g), chopped**

**1 tablespoon fresh basil, chopped**

**1 tablespoon fresh oregano, chopped**

**Seasoning salt**

**1 tablespoon sugar**

**Crushed red pepper**

**1 cup (180 g) canned butter beans**

**2 cups (240 g) chopped or sliced carrots**

**1 large potato (370 g), diced**

**1½ cups (220 g) corn kernels**

**2 cups (220 g) green beans**

**1½ cups (170 g) sliced or diced yellow squash**

**1½ cups (170 g) sliced or diced zucchini**

In a large pot over medium heat, cook the tomatoes with the onion, bell pepper, basil, oregano, seasoning salt to taste, sugar, and crushed red pepper to taste for 20 minutes.

Add the butter beans, carrots, and potato. Cook for 5 minutes.

Add the corn, green beans, yellow squash, and zucchini. Cook for 5 more minutes. The total cooking time should be about 30 minutes, unless the vegetables are still too crunchy—if so, then cook for 5 minutes longer.

**TIP: If the base of the soup is too thin, thicken by mixing 1 teaspoon cornstarch with ⅓ cup (75 ml) water. Stir the mixture into the soup at the end of cooking and continue to cook for a few minutes longer to thicken.**

# She Crab Soup

SERVES: 8 TO 10

RICH, HEARTY, AND FLAVORFUL, SHE CRAB SOUP IS A FAMILY AND REGIONAL FAVORITE. Named for the female crab "roe" found in many versions of the bisque-like dish, she crab soup is served in homes and restaurants throughout the Lowcountry, including the South Carolina and Georgia coasts. I made this favorite for the Dodge family—who loved their soup with a dash of sherry—and my own family, who enjoyed this at celebrations or during holidays. She crab soup is a rich soup, and it's meant to be enjoyed with the ones you love. Oyster crackers, warm homemade biscuits (page 214), or Tam Tam crackers make great sides because they don't overpower the soup's delicate crab flavor.

**1 cup (150 g) cooked long-grain white rice, plus ½ cup (125 g) more if needed**

**2 cups (480 ml) whole milk, plus ½ cup (120 ml) more if needed**

**2 cups (480 ml) half-and-half**

**½ teaspoon ground mace**

**1½ teaspoons Nature's Seasons**

**Salt, to taste**

**¼ cup (½ stick/55 g) unsalted butter**

**1 cup (100 g) diced celery**

**2 pounds (910 g) crabmeat**

**½ cup (120 ml) sherry, for serving (optional)**

**Scallions, thinly sliced, for garnish (optional)**

Place the cooked rice, 1 cup (240 ml) of the milk, and 1 cup (240 ml) of the half-and-half in a blender. Blend until it becomes a thick, smooth mixture.

Bring about 2 quarts (2 L) water to a boil in a large pot. Place a large steel mixing bowl over the pot of boiling water. Do not let the bottom of the mixing bowl touch the boiling water (you may use a double boiler if you have one). Reduce the heat to medium. In the steel bowl or double boiler, combine the rice mixture and the remaining 1 cup (240 ml) each of whole milk and half-and-half. Add the mace, Nature's Seasons, and salt. Stir the mixture, taste, and add more seasoning if needed. The mixture should be thick, like a bisque. If it's not thick enough, blend about ½ cup (100 g ) additional cooked rice and ½ cup (120 ml) additional milk together and add it to the mixture.

In a medium skillet, melt the butter. Sauté the celery for 3 minutes over medium heat, retaining its green color. Add the celery to the soup. Taste the soup, and add seasoning as needed.

Fold the crabmeat into the soup. Do not stir, because that will break up the crabmeat. Three or four folding movements should do the trick.

Transfer the soup to a separate large pot and cook over low heat for 7 to 10 minutes. Serve. If you're using sherry, guests can pour the sherry over their soup to their liking.

# Beef Stew

SERVES: 8 TO 10

THE RICH, SAVORY BROTH OF THIS STEW IS SO WARM AND COMFORTING, BUT THE CUTS OF BEEF DO THEIR PART, TOO. Beef stew can be served year-round, but it's especially nice during the colder months, thanks to its hearty texture and rich flavor. Serve the stew over noodles or white rice, and garnish with just a bit of parsley.

**2½ pounds (1.2 kg) beef stewing meat**

**Seasoning salt, to taste**

**2½ tablespoons all-purpose flour**

**3 tablespoons bacon drippings or olive oil**

**5 cups (1.2 L) water**

**1 large onion (225 g), diced**

**½ bell pepper (60 g), diced**

**1 rib celery, diced**

**½ pound (225 g) baby carrots or carrot sticks (optional)**

**1 pound (455 g) yellow or white potatoes, roughly chopped (optional)**

Rinse the beef and pat dry with paper towels. Season with seasoning salt to taste, then sprinkle with the flour.

Pour the bacon drippings into a large, heavy-bottomed pot and place over medium heat. Add the stew beef and brown it for about 3 minutes.

Add the water, onion, bell pepper, and celery. Bring to a boil. Turn the heat down and simmer for about 2 hours, until the beef is tender.

Add carrots and potatoes, as desired. Cook over low heat for another 15 minutes.

*"Everybody that's stirrin' a pot's not cookin'. Do the cookin' instead."*

# 5 | GRITS, GRAINS, BISCUITS & BREADS

BREAD IS THE STAFF OF LIFE. GRAINS HAVE SHAPED EVERY SINGLE GROUP OF PEOPLE IN THE WORLD SINCE THE BEGINNING OF TIME. The food that we love—pasta, bread, rice, and more—come from grains. When the Gullah Geechee people were brought to the Sea Islands, they were known as the experts in growing and using grains in the Lowcountry.

Our history with grains, like most of our history, goes back to Africa. Many of our Gullah Geechee ancestors came from rice-growing regions in West Africa. When enslaved people were brought to the United States, they brought this knowledge and skill to plantations across the South, but especially in the Carolinas. Gullah Geechee people developed advanced systems and grew rice in large quantities. Carolina Gold rice, a starchy, sticky long-grain rice, became the gold mine of the South. It built South Carolina's wealth—white South Carolina's wealth. Sometimes I would wonder how these white folks could build such big houses, and why their property cost so much. I would wonder, where did they get that money from? They got that money from us, from Black folks. Many of us can't get that kind of money. We work a lifetime and we still ain't gon' get it, even though we work harder for it.

Our hard work created southern culture and food. After slavery, some of the newly freed Gullah Geechee people continued growing rice and grains, and we shared our rice dishes with the region. Mama, my grandmother, worked at the Mitchell Place Plantation. There was a line drawn between their rice and our rice. There was a pond at the plantation, and Mama and other Black folks who worked on the plantation used to plant on that pond. Mama and them could plant vegetables and things like that. They made that land their own.

On that land, we grew the grains that sustained us. We had a grain every day. If we didn't have it in the morning, we had it in the afternoon when we came home from school. Some of the most famous dishes in the Lowcountry, like red rice (page 213), hoppin' John (page 207), and chicken perloo (page 210), are straight from the Gullah Geechee people. This was Black folks' food, food that Mama made all the time. Now people come down here just to get a taste of what we've been eating for generations. Our culture took grits, made from crushed and ground corn, and turned them into something real special. Now the shrimp and grits we used to eat before we went to work are on brunch menus across the South. Not only did we build this region's wealth, we gave the Lowcountry some of its most treasured dishes, too.

In this chapter, I share the rice, bread, grits, and pasta recipes that Mama used to cook, and that I grew up cooking for my family and community. These meals show a lot about our history and food traditions. I cooked some of these very dishes for my husband and children, and for the people I worked for around Edisto Island. They brought warmth and comfort to our home and community. I hope they do the same for you, too.

***"Lunch was my favorite part because she made sure that, if we didn't have sandwiches, she would make those biscuits. We would eat the Sally Long or Johnny Long bread, as she would call it. And it was good."*** —MY DAUGHTER ELIZANN MACK

Silver Wing

ISSAQUEENA

CORN MEAL

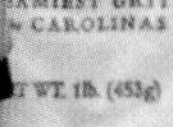

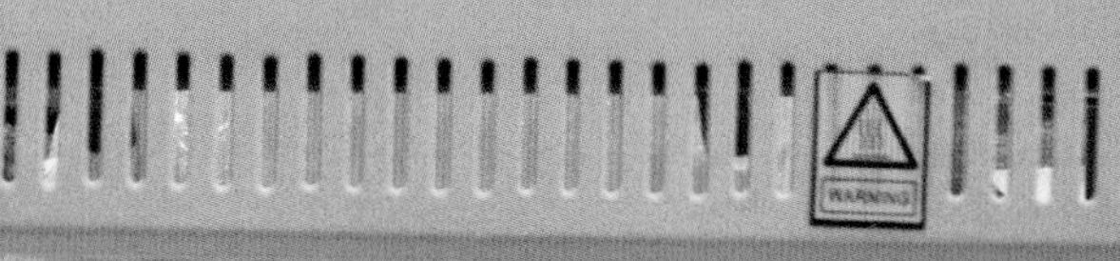
WARNING
WARNING

5-24-21

# Baked Cheese Grits

SERVES: 4 TO 6

IN THE UNITED STATES, WE CAN THANK THE MUSKOGEE TRIBE FOR LAYING THE FOUNDATION FOR WHAT WE NOW KNOW AS GRITS. There are so many ways to serve grits, and one of my favorites is by adding cheese, which turns this porridge into a mouth-watering soufflé. I don't believe in wasting food, so I would use leftover Jim Dandy grits to make this dish for my loved ones. Enjoy this baked dish for breakfast with bacon or sausage or add it as a side to fried fish (page 63) for a South Carolinian take on breakfast-for-dinner.

**1½ cups (425 g) grits, preferably Jim Dandy or coarse-grind grits**

**½ cup (120 ml) Carnation evaporated milk or half-and-half**

**4 tablespoons unsalted butter, divided**

**1 cup (115 g) grated sharp cheddar cheese, plus ½ cup (55 g) for the top of the casserole**

**½ teaspoon salt**

**2 large eggs, beaten**

Preheat the oven to 350°F (170°C). Grease a 9 by 13-inch (23 by 33 cm) baking dish with 1 tablespoon of butter.

Cook the grits according to the package instructions. Add the evaporated milk, butter, 1 cup (115 g) of the cheese, the salt, and eggs, mixing well with a spoon.

Pour the mixture into the baking dish. Sprinkle the top of the grits with the remaining cheese.

Bake for 30 to 45 minutes. The grits should be like a thick porridge and should not be runny. Check the grits with a knife or fork to determine when the dish is done.

# Stone-Ground Grits

SERVES: 4 TO 6

THE GRAININESS OF GRITS ARE SMOOTHED OVER IN THIS SLOW-COOKED DISH. Stone-ground grits work best here, because they have fewer "eyeballs," as I like to call them, or "specks." The eyeballs come from the cob, and shouldn't be in there. To prepare your grits, you want to first rinse them, drain them of any water, and repeat the process three or four times until you remove the eyeballs. If using regular grits, I've found that Jim Dandy grits have less specks than Quaker grits, but you can use whichever brand you like.

**1½ cups (260 g) stone-ground grits**

**2 cups (480 ml) tepid water, plus more as needed**

**½ cup (120 ml) chicken broth**

**½ cup (120 ml) heavy cream**

**1 teaspoon salt**

In a deep 12-inch (30.5 cm) skillet, combine the grits, water, broth, cream, and salt. Stir the mixture and bring it to a boil over high heat. Reduce the heat to low and allow the mixture to simmer for about 15 minutes, until all of the liquid is absorbed. If the mixture is too thin, more dry grits can be added to the mixture to thicken it while it is cooking. Be sure to stir the mixture. Turn down the temperature to low heat and cook until done, at least 1 hour.

## *GRITS ON EDISTO ISLAND*

For yellow and white grits, we had to shell the corn off the cob, put it in those big hundred-pound sacks, and then take that to Jericho. They'd process it and send it back. And when they send it back, you got a twenty-five- or forty-five-pound bag white grits, and a ten- or fifteen-pound bag of the husks. The yellow grits was the same. The husks all came back too, and went to the hog.

We'd plant our own corn. My uncle would plant it around April. When we were little we couldn't go out there, but when we got bigger they'd show us how to drop the corn in the row. Maybe ten here, ten somewhere else. They had a lot of corn. They needed it to grind, and also for the horse, cow, and the hogs. We harvested in August, September, October. Back then there was no sweet corn. You ate the same corn as the horse.

# Baked Garlic or Cheese Leftover Grits

SERVES: 4 TO 6

MAKING A BIG POT OF GRITS OFTEN CREATES LEFTOVERS. Instead of wasting perfectly good grits, this dish is how I put them to use. Whether you decide to use garlic or cheese is really a matter of preference, and you should also feel free to use both. Serve grits with poached or scrambled eggs and bacon.

**At least 6 cups (1.5 kg) leftover grits**

**3 garlic cloves, crushed; or 1 cup (115 g) grated cheddar cheese**

**2 large eggs, beaten**

**Salt and pepper**

**¼ cup (25 g) breadcrumbs, or ¼ cup (30 g) grated cheese**

**Paprika**

Preheat the oven to 350°F (170°C). Grease a 9 by 13-inch (23 by 33 cm) baking dish.

In a large bowl, combine the grits with the garlic or 1 cup (115 g) cheese, the eggs, and salt and pepper to taste. Pour into the prepared baking dish. Bake for 20 to 25 minutes.

Sprinkle the top of the casserole with the breadcrumbs or cheese.

Preheat your oven's broiler to 500°F (260°C), or its highest setting. Once heated, place the grits under the broiler and cook until golden. Garnish with paprika.

*"When you grow up, it's a community thing. Nobody in the community went hungry. You would look out for each other. It was just a great blessing, working together, doing things together, taking care of the kids. It's what we did back then."* —M.P.

# Fried Grits

SERVES: 4 TO 6

THESE FRIED GRITS ARE LIKE SMALL CAKE SLICES. Golden brown on the outside and piping hot on the inside, fried grits are a great side dish at breakfast, lunch, or dinner.

**2 cups (340 g) yellow or white grits**

**1 large egg, beaten**

**½ cup (120 ml) milk, whole or 2%**

**½ cup (65 g) all-purpose flour**

**½ cup (1 stick/115 g) unsalted butter**

**¼ cup (60 ml) vegetable oil**

Cook the grits according to the package instructions.

Spray a 5 by 9-inch (12 by 23 cm) loaf pan with cooking spray. Pour the cooked grits into the pan. Refrigerate until cold. Grits can also be cooked in the morning and refrigerated, and will be ready to fry for supper.

Remove the grits from the pan and place on a cutting board. The grits should be a firm loaf. Cut the grits into slices a little thicker than a slice of bread. Set aside.

In a mixing bowl, beat the egg, then add the milk and stir together. One at a time, place the grits slices into the bowl and coat with the egg mixture. Be careful not to break the slices.

Sprinkle flour lightly on a piece of waxed paper. Place the slices on the floured paper. Then sprinkle the top of each slice with flour.

In a cast-iron skillet, melt the butter over medium-high heat, then add the oil. The oil will prevent the butter from burning.

Place the sliced grits in the butter and oil and cook for about 2 minutes on each side, until golden brown. Cook over medium-high heat so the slices will not burn.

# Macaroni and Cheese

SERVES: 8 TO 10

WE ALL NEED TO THANK JAMES HEMINGS, THE AMERICAN-BORN, FRENCH-TRAINED CHEF WHO INTRODUCED MACARONI AND CHEESE TO THE AMERICAN FOODWAYS. Enslaved by Thomas Jefferson, Hemings used his French training and knowledge of American crops and ingredients to create one of the most cherished dishes in the country.

I believe that macaroni and cheese should be creamy, cheesy, and just a little bit sweet. A can of Carnation milk and generous use of cheddar cheese does the trick.

**½ cup (1 stick/115 g) plus 1 tablespoon unsalted butter**

**1 (16-ounce/455 g) box dried macaroni or elbows pasta**

**2 tablespoons mustard**

**1 (12-ounce/354 ml) can Carnation evaporated milk or 1 cup (240 ml) heavy cream**

**3 cups (720 ml) milk, whole or 2%, plus more if needed**

**1 cup (115 g) shredded medium or sharp cheddar cheese, plus ½ cup (55 g) for the top of the casserole**

**2 large eggs, lightly beaten**

**½ teaspoon salt**

Preheat the oven to 350°F (170°C). Grease a 9 by 13-inch (23 by 33 cm) baking dish with 1 tablespoon of butter.

Cook the macaroni until al dente, according to the package instructions. Drain well.

Add the butter, mustard, evaporated milk, and 1 cup (240 ml) of the regular milk to the macaroni, and stir to combine. Add 1 cup (115 g) of the cheese and the eggs, and mix again. Finally, add salt to the pasta mixture, and mix again.

Pour the mixture into the baking dish. Pour the remaining milk evenly on top of the mixture, covering the entire dish with milk. If any pasta is uncovered, add more milk as needed.

Sprinkle the macaroni with the remaining cheese. Bake the casserole for 45 to 50 minutes, until the top is browned.

# Dirty Rice

SERVES: 10

ONE-POT RICE DISHES ARE DEEPLY ROOTED IN WEST AFRICAN COOKING. Dirty rice is yet another dish that is well seasoned, well cooked, and comes together in just one pot, making it an easy and sure-to-satisfy dish to serve to large groups of people. The pork sausage adds a sweet and savory flavor, and the rice gets a nice velvety texture thanks to the fat from the pork and bacon drippings.

**4 slices bacon**

**1 (16-ounce/455 g) package loose pork sausage**

**1 large onion, diced**

**1 bell pepper, diced**

**4½ cups (1 L) tepid water**

**1 tablespoon Nature's Seasons**

**1 teaspoon crushed red pepper**

**1½ teaspoons soy sauce**

**1 teaspoon Kitchen Bouquet (optional)**

**3½ cups (645 g) long-grain white rice, rinsed**

In a large, heavy-bottomed pot, cook the bacon over high heat until crisp. Remove the bacon—but not the oil and drippings—from the pot and allow the bacon to cool. Once cooled, cut the bacon into small pieces and set aside.

Meanwhile, roll the sausage into small balls. Heat the same cooking pot, and cook the sausage in the bacon drippings until browned, about 5 minutes. Add the onion and bell pepper to the sausage and sauté for another 5 minutes.

Return the bacon to the pot, and add the water. Bring the mixture to a boil. Reduce the heat to medium, then add the Nature's Seasons, crushed red pepper, soy sauce, and Kitchen Bouquet, if using. Return the mixture to a boil and cook for 2 minutes.

Add the rice and stir with a fork. Reduce the heat to low and cook until most of the water has been absorbed, about 30 minutes. If using a steamer, fill the bottom halfway with water, transfer the rice mixture to the top of the steamer, cover, and steam for 20 to 25 minutes, or until done.

## *BACK THEN, WE HAD OUR OWN RICE POND*

It was right there by the house on the Mitchell plantation. On Friday afternoons, Mama would say, "You gotta get up early and get that rice if we want it for Sunday dinner." And when we were small, my uncle would go out there with us, and we would hold this sheet, and he would just shake it in that sheet—Marion would have one end and I'd have the other.

When we'd get enough, then we'd bring it home in a bag. They had a table outside, and Mama had a rolling pin that she made herself. She would put the rice in a bag and roll it and roll it, back and forth, back and forth, until we get the hull off. Then she'd put it in a pan, and put a big washing tub on the ground. She'd stick that pan down in there, and she would whistle for the breeze to come—and the wind would come and blow the hull off. Then she'd go back, put it in the pan again, and we'd do it the second or third time, and you'd have no hull. And we'd do it just like that with the peas and beans, too.

See, the rice back then from the lower part of the land would be like the brown rice now. It was never white like it is now. The rice then was red rice—no processing or nothing. Now it's white as chalk.

# Hoppin' John

SERVES: 10

THERE'S A LOT OF CONFUSION SURROUNDING HOPPIN' JOHN. People confuse it with black-eyed peas and rice, another dish that many Americans, especially Black folks, enjoy on or near New Year's Day. In the Lowcountry, we make hoppin' John, a one-pot rice dish, using field peas, which are red-brown in color, and are slightly sweet and nutty. Field peas and black-eyed peas are both types of cowpeas, but they're used for different dishes and offer their own special flavors.

My husband loved him some hoppin' John. It was the only thing he'd eat leftovers of. He just couldn't get enough. Like many of my one-pot rice dishes, I use salt pork as the primary source of flavor. Here, I also use bacon. They used to say, if you use smoked neck bone instead of bacon and mix pinto beans, speckled lima beans, and field peas together in your hoppin' John, you'll bite your finger! So to this day, I make it the old way.

1 pound (455 g) dried field peas, cow peas, or crowder peas

2 (14-ounce/400 g) smoked ham hocks, sliced into 1-inch pieces

3 cups (375 g) chopped onion, divided

½ pound (225 g) bacon

½ pound (225 g) salt pork, cut into 1-inch (2.5 cm) chunks

1 teaspoon Nature's Seasons, plus more to taste

3 cups (720 ml) water

Crushed red pepper, to taste

3 cups (555 g) long-grain white rice, unrinsed

Rinse the dried peas two or three times, removing all dirt stones.

In a large pot, add the cleaned peas, smoked ham hocks, 1 cup (125 g) of the onion, and 2½ quarts (2.4 L) water to boil. Once the mixture is boiling, reduce the heat to medium-low and cook the peas for at least 1 hour. The peas should be tender, but not too soft. Once the peas are cooked, drain and set aside.

In a separate large, heavy-bottomed pot, cook the bacon over high heat until crisp. Remove the bacon—but not the oil and drippings—from the pot and allow the bacon to cool. Once cooled, cut the bacon into small pieces and set aside.

Heat the same cooking pot, and cook the salt pork in the bacon drippings until browned, about 5 minutes. Add the remaining 2 cups (250 g) onion and sauté for another 5 to 7 minutes. Do not drain. Add the field peas mixture.

Return the bacon to the pot and add the Nature's Seasons, water, and a dash of crushed red pepper. Bring the mixture to a boil and cook for 5 minutes. Taste this mixture; add more seasoning if desired. Reduce the heat to medium.

Add the uncooked rice. Stir the mixture with a fork and make sure you can feel the heaviness of the rice—then you know you have enough rice in comparison to the amount of liquid.

Allow the rice and peas mixture to cook, uncovered, until most of the water is absorbed, 8 to 10 minutes.

If using a steamer, transfer the absorbed mixture to the steamer and cover. (If too dry, sprinkle a little water over the top of the mixture and cook for 10 to 15 minutes more.) If using the regular pot, continue to cook over low heat for about 15 minutes, or until all the water has been absorbed.

# Hushpuppies

SERVES: 6 TO 8

MOST PEOPLE RECOGNIZE HUSHPUPPIES AS THE CAN'T-MISS SIDE FOR FRIED FISH AND OTHER TYPES OF SEAFOOD. I'm one of those people—I enjoy eating hushpuppies with any fried seafood dish. These crisped balls of cornmeal are a lot like cornbread, but their perfectly soft interior and crispy exterior separates these from other cornmeal-based sides. Mine are similar to what you'd find in a southern restaurant.

**1 large egg, beaten**

**2 tablespoons sugar**

**1 cup (240 ml) vegetable oil, plus 2 cups (480 ml) for frying**

**½ cup (65 g) all-purpose flour**

**1 teaspoon salt**

**2 cups (270 g) yellow cornmeal**

**2½ teaspoons baking powder**

**1¼ cups (300 ml) milk, whole or 2%**

**1 cup (110 g) grated onion**

**½ cup (45 g) chopped bell pepper**

**¼ teaspoon cayenne pepper**

In a large mixing bowl, use a spoon to beat together the egg, sugar, and 1 cup (240 ml) of the oil.

Add the flour, salt, cornmeal, and baking powder. Mix well.

Add the milk and mix. Add the onion, bell pepper, and cayenne pepper. Mix the ingredients together until well combined.

In a large skillet, heat 2 cups (480 ml) oil over high heat. Once the oil is shimmering, reduce the heat to medium. In batches, take heaping tablespoons of the cornmeal mixture and drop them in the oil. Cook for 3 to 4 minutes, until golden brown. You'll know they're done when the hushpuppies float. Drain the hushpuppies on a plate covered with a paper towel, and serve.

# Chicken Perloo

SERVES: 8 TO 10

MANY OF THE ONE-POT RICE DISHES IN THE LOWCOUNTRY AND THE SOUTH CAN TRACE THEIR ORIGINS BACK TO WEST AFRICA. There's jollof rice in West Africa, jambalaya in Louisiana, and here in the Lowcountry? We've got red rice and chicken perloo. Chicken perloo has a lot of the same western European and African cooking styles you find in dishes like Spanish paella and Ghanaian jollof rice. However, tender chicken, ambrosial stock, and perfectly fluffed rice make this a true Lowcountry dish.



**6 tablespoons (90 ml) bacon grease or vegetable oil**

**½ pound (225 g) salt pork, cut into 1-inch (2.5 cm) chunks**

**1 cup (125 g) roughly chopped onion**

**5 cups (1.2 L) chicken broth**

**1 teaspoon Nature's Seasons**

**1 teaspoon poultry seasoning**

**1 pound (455 g) cooked chicken thighs, skin removed and roughly chopped**

**2½ cups (460 g) long-grain white rice, unrinsed**

In a large, heavy-bottomed pot, heat 2 tablespoons of the bacon grease or oil over high heat. Once the grease or oil is shimmering, add the salt pork and cook on high heat for 1 minute. Pour the remaining bacon grease or oil into the pot. Reduce the heat to medium-low and cook the salt pork for about 5 minutes, until browned.

Once browned, remove the salt pork from the pot and set aside. Leave enough oil to coat the bottom of the pot. Add the onion and fry for 1 minute. Return the cooked salt pork to the pot and cook the onion and salt pork together over low heat for about 5 minutes, until onion just darkens.

Add the broth, Nature's Seasons, and poultry seasoning and bring to a boil.

Once boiling, add the chicken. Cook for about 2 minutes, then add the rice. Adjust the heat to medium-low and cook until most of the liquid has been absorbed, 10 to 15 minutes.

If using a steamer, transfer the rice mixture to the top of the steamer, cover, and steam over medium heat for about 20 minutes, until done. If you're using the regular pot, continue to cook the rice mixture on medium-low heat for 20 to 25 minutes, until the rice has absorbed all of the broth. Once done, stir the rice with a fork, and serve immediately.

# Red Rice

SERVES: 8 TO 10

RED RICE GOES BACK TO THE OLD, OLD DAYS—THE DAYS BEFORE ME, MY MOMMA, AND HERS. It's a rich one-pot rice dish twith roots in African culinary traditions. Sometimes called Charleston red rice, this dish owes a great debt to the enslaved Africans who brought their knowledge of rice and vegetable farming to the United States. Here on Edisto, Wednesdays and Fridays were seafood days. We had shrimp or fish with red rice, so it was something to look forward to.

Gullah Geechee red rice is one of the best dishes you can enjoy. Now, red rice can be a tricky thing. If you don't have enough rice, it will come out like mush. If you have too much rice, you can add water, but the texture will be uneven. Early in the cooking, you want to use your spoon to feel the weight of the rice, and make sure it's cooking evenly.

Don't let this dish intimidate you—with well-seasoned vegetables, slices of sausage, and perfectly cooked rice, you've just about got yourself a meal. Oh, and when you put some fatback in there? Now you're talking.

**½ pound (225 g) salt pork, cut into 1-inch (2.5 cm) chunks**

**1 large onion, chopped**

**1 large bell pepper, chopped**

**½ cup (50 g) chopped celery**

**3 smoked sausages (about 14 ounces/395 g)**

**1 (6-ounce/170 g) can tomato paste**

**1 teaspoon crushed red pepper**

**1½ teaspoons Nature's Seasons, plus more to taste**

**2 cups (370 g) long-grain white rice, unrinsed**

Fry the salt pork in a large pot over medium heat until browned, 8 to 10 minutes. Add the onion, bell pepper, and celery and cook until tender, 5 to 7 minutes.

Cut the sausage into bite-size pieces and add to the pot; cook until lightly browned, about 5 minutes. Stir in the tomato paste and 5 cups (1.2 L) water and bring to a boil over high heat. Add the crushed red pepper and Nature's Seasons and stir. Taste and add more seasoning if needed.

Add the rice. Cook, stirring frequently to keep the rice from sticking, until most of the liquid has been absorbed and the rice is tender, about 10 minutes.

If using a rice steamer, transfer the absorbed mixture to the steamer. Cover the steamer, and cook on low heat for 15 to 20 minutes, or until all of the liquid is absorbed and the rice can be fluffed with a fork. If using a pot, cover the pot and cook over the lowest possible heat, stirring with a fork as needed, for 25 to 30 minutes, or until the rice has absorbed all the liquid.

# Biscuits from Scratch

SERVES: 9 OR 10; MAKES: 18 TO 20 SMALL OR 9 OR 10 LARGE

A MORNING BISCUIT, PERFECTLY CRISPED AND GOLDEN ON THE OUTSIDE AND WARM AND FLAKY ON THE INSIDE, IS SURE TO START THE DAY OFF RIGHT. I learned to make these from a cook named Ms. Brown. She would press down on the crust to see if it would spring back. If it didn't, or if the taste wasn't just right, she'd throw them away. I did this day after day until they were perfect.

Biscuits take practice, so if the texture isn't right on the first try, try it again. The secret to making good biscuits? When you're rolling the biscuit dough, don't fool with the dough too much—it will make them come out tough. You want to mix and roll the dough just enough so it's combined, but not overly prepped. The number of biscuits from this recipe depends on the size of the cutter (18 to 20 for a small cutter, 9 or 10 for a large cutter).



**1 cup (205 g) Crisco shortening**

**1 large egg**

**2 to 4 tablespoons sugar, plus more to taste**

**1½ cups (360 ml) milk, whole or 2%**

**3⅓ cups (415 g) self-rising flour, preferably White Lily, plus more as needed, plus 1 cup (125 g) for the counter and shaping**

Preheat the oven to 350°F (170°C).

In a mixing bowl, using a spoon, mix together the Crisco, egg, and sugar until smooth. Add sugar according to desired sweetness.

Stir in the milk until the Crisco mixture is broken up a bit, then stir in the 3½ cups (415 g) flour. Mix until just combined.

Use the remaining flour for dusting the countertop, biscuit cutter, and dough: Sprinkle ⅓ cup (40 g) evenly onto the countertop where the biscuits will be rolled out. Scrape the dough onto the flour, then sprinkle ⅓ cup (40 g) on top of the dough so it will not stick to your hands. Pat the dough with your palms into a slab about ¾ inch (2 cm) thick. Put ⅓ cup (40 g) flour in a small bowl or a pile on the side to dip the biscuit cutter into.

Dip a biscuit cutter or the top of a small cup into flour. Cut biscuits and place on ungreased cookie sheets, leaving just a bit of dough between each cut. (Use a metal spatula to transfer the biscuits to the cookie sheets, if necessary. They will be very delicate.)

Bake for 35 to 40 minutes, until golden brown.

# Cornbread Stuffing

SERVES: 12 TO 14

A GOOD CORNBREAD STUFFING KEEPS FLUFFY PIECES OF THE BREAD INTACT. You don't want a cornbread stuffing that's so soupy you can't taste the cornbread. To achieve that consistency, replace the common wooden mixing spoon with a fork to combine the cornbread with herbs and softer, juicier ingredients.

**1 large egg**

**3 tablespoons Crisco shortening**

**1 tablespoon sugar**

**1½ cups (190 g) self-rising flour**

**2½ cups (450 g) white cornmeal**

**2 cups (480 ml) milk, whole or 2%**

**1 pound (455 g) chicken giblets: liver, gizzard, and/or neck**

**4 cups (960 ml) tepid water**

**1 teaspoon Nature's Seasons**

**1 tablespoon poultry seasoning**

**½ cup (1 stick/115 g) unsalted butter**

**1 cup (125 g) diced onion**

**1 cup (100 g) diced celery**

**1 (14½-ounce/411 g) can chicken broth, if necessary**

Preheat the oven to 350°F (170°C). Grease a 9 by 13-inch (23 by 33 cm) baking dish that's 2 inches (5 cm) deep.

In a large bowl, beat together the egg, Crisco, and sugar. Add the flour, cornmeal, and milk. Mix well.

Pour into the prepared baking dish and bake for 35 to 40 minutes, until golden brown.

While the cornbread is baking, boil the giblets in the water seasoned with Nature's Seasons and poultry seasoning until done, about 1 hour. Save the liquid and allow it to cool. Cut the giblets into small pieces.

In a 12-inch (30.5 cm) cast-iron skillet, melt the butter over low heat. Add the onion and celery and sauté until tender, 5 to 7 minutes.

Once the cornbread is done, allow it to cool. When cooled, break up the cornbread and place it in a large mixing bowl. Add the giblets, onion, and celery. Use a fork to stir until everything is mixed together. Do not stir with a wooden spoon.

Add the cooking liquid (about 2½ cups/600 ml) from the giblets to the mixture. If there is not enough liquid, add canned broth as needed. The mixture should be very moist, but not soupy.

Bake in an ungreased casserole dish until golden brown, 20 to 25 minutes.

# Cornbread or Cornbread Muffins

SERVES: 10 TO 12

THIS RECIPE CAN GIVE YOU WARM CORNBREAD, OR CORNBREAD MUFFINS—IT'S UP TO YOU HOW TO USE THE BATTER. To get a bright golden color, I prefer using yellow cornmeal over white. Be careful not to use a cornmeal mix—plain cornmeal is essential to get this recipe just right.

**1¼ cups (300 ml) milk, whole or 2%**

**2 large eggs**

**3 heaping tablespoons Crisco shortening**

**1 tablespoon sugar, or more if you like your cornbread sweet**

**1½ cups (190 g) self-rising flour**

**1½ cups (205 g) yellow cornmeal**

Preheat the oven to 350°F (170°C). Grease a 9-inch (23 cm) square baking pan or a 12-cup muffin tin with cooking spray.

Using a spoon, mix all the ingredients together in a mixing bowl. Pour the mixture into the prepared baking pan or muffin tin.

Bake for 30 to 35 minutes, until golden brown.

# Oatmeal

SERVES: 2 TO 4

OATMEAL DOESN'T HAVE TO BE BORING. Adding a bit of dairy gives the oats some heft, and with the right toppings, oatmeal can be a healthy breakfast to look forward to.

**½ cup (45 g) old-fashioned oats**

**1 teaspoon butter**

**Milk, heavy cream, or sour cream, for serving**

**Ground cinnamon, brown sugar, raisins, walnuts, pecans, and/or cut-up apple for toppings**

Combine the oats, 1 cup (240 ml) water, and butter in the top of a double boiler over simmering water. Cook over medium-high heat for 8 to 10 minutes, until soft and thickened,

Serve with milk, heavy cream, or sour cream as desired.

Add cinnamon, brown sugar, raisins, walnuts, pecans, and/or apple for variety.

# Pancakes and Syrup

SERVES: 8 TO 10

PANCAKES AND SYRUP IS ONE OF THOSE DISHES THAT SEEMS LIKE IT'S ALWAYS JUST BEEN THERE. I remember eating pancakes as a child, and everywhere I went, from work, to marriage, to parenthood, it was always a breakfast dish that everyone seemed to love. I flip my pancakes just once to avoid overly cooking and burning these fluffy discs of goodness. Pancakes are perfectly fine plain, but you can change them up by adding cooked rice, or oatmeal, raisins, pecans, blueberries, bananas, or strawberries, and you can add one or more depending on your taste. Serve with melted butter and warm syrup—which I'll give you my secret recipe for.

FOR THE PANCAKES:

**1 large egg, beaten**

**2 to 3 tablespoons sugar**

**3 cups (375 g) self-rising flour, preferably White Lily**

**2 cups (480 ml) milk, whole or 2%, plus ½ to ⅓ cup (120 to 160 ml) more if needed**

**1 cup (205 g) Crisco shortening, melted**

**Optional: ½ cup (125 g) cooked rice or oatmeal, raisins, pecans, blueberries, bananas, or strawberries to taste**

FOR THE SYRUP:

**2 cups syrup, preferably Country Kitchen syrup or Karo corn syrup**

**¼ cup (½ stick/55 g) unsalted butter**

Make the pancakes: In a large mixing bowl, combine the egg and sugar.

Add the flour and 2 cups (480 ml) of the milk. Do not beat; stir gently. Add the melted Crisco. Continue to gently stir until mixed and the dry ingredients are absorbed.

Because the Crisco will "stiffen" the batter, add additional milk as needed—just enough so the mixture is not too loose and not too thick. Gently stir in any optional ingredients.

Heat an electric pancake griddle to 350°F (170°C). Do not grease the griddle. Spoon the batter onto the griddle to the desired pancake size.

Brown the first side and then flip the pancakes and brown the second side. Serve immediately.

Make the syrup: In a small saucepan, heat the syrup over medium-high heat. Once warm, add the butter and allow the butter to melt in the pot. Stir together until combined. Remove from the stove. Drizzle on top of pancakes and/or waffles.

**TIP: If using all-purpose flour instead of self-rising, add ½ teaspoon salt and 1 teaspoon baking powder per 1 cup (125 g) all-purpose flour. For this recipe, if using all-purpose flour, add 1½ teaspoons salt and 3 teaspoons baking powder.**

# Popovers

SERVES: 12

POPOVERS MIGHT LOOK DIFFICULT TO MAKE, BUT IT'S REALLY ABOUT HAVING THE RIGHT PAN, AND PAYING ATTENTION TO THE TIME. These popovers are fluffy, eggy, and expansive as can be on the inside, and crisp and golden on the outside. These cloudlike treats are baked best in a standard popover pan, where the batter can bake up and out, but if one isn't available, a muffin tins works as an alternative.

**3 large eggs**

**1 cup (240 ml) milk, whole or 2%**

**2 teaspoons vegetable oil**

**½ teaspoon salt**

**1 teaspoon sugar**

**1 cup (125 g) all-purpose flour**

Preheat the oven to 450°F (230°C). Grease a popover pan with cooking spray.

In a large mixing bowl, beat the eggs with an electric mixer.

Add the milk, oil, salt, sugar, and flour and beat the mixture until just combined. Be careful not to overbeat.

Heat the pan in the oven, carefully remove it, and fill each mold halfway with batter. Return to the oven and bake for 30 minutes. Remove the pan from the oven and adjust the oven temperature to 350°F (170°C).

Pierce the popovers with a toothpick to release the steam. Return the popovers to the oven and bake for 10 more minutes.

*"I am the living bread that came down from heaven. Whoever eats this bread will live forever. This bread is my flesh, which I will give for the life of the world."* —JOHN 6:51

# Spoon Bread

SERVES: 8 TO 12

YOU DON'T SEE SPOON BREAD ON TOO MANY TABLES ANYMORE, BUT YOU SHOULD. A cross between a casserole and a pudding, spoon bread goes great on a plate with shrimp, coleslaw, sliced tomatoes, and fresh broccoli. Make sure you don't open the oven door while it's cooking, though—you don't want your bread to fall!

**2 cups (240 g) self-rising cornmeal, coarse or fine**

**½ cup (1 stick/115 g) unsalted butter**

**2½ cups (600 ml) tepid water**

**1 teaspoon salt**

**4 large eggs**

**3½ cups (840 ml) whole milk**

**1 teaspoon sugar**

Preheat the oven to 350°F (170°C). Spray a 9 by 13-inch (23 by 33 cm) baking dish with cooking spray of your choice.

In a large, heavy-bottomed pot, combine the cornmeal, butter, water, and salt. Cook over high heat for 6 to 8 minutes, until all the water is absorbed.

Set the mixture aside to cool. Separate the eggs.

In a mixing bowl, mix together the egg yolks, milk, and sugar with a wooden spoon. Add this to the cornmeal mixture. Mix well.

In a separate bowl, beat the egg whites with an electric mixer on high speed until fluffy.

Gently fold the egg whites into the cornmeal mixture. Pour into the baking dish.

Bake for 35 to 40 minutes. Do not open the oven door until ready to serve. Opening the oven door will cause the spoon bread to fall. Serve immediately.

# Waffles

SERVES: 10

MY CHILDREN KNOW HOW IMPORTANT BREAKFAST IS IN MY HOUSEHOLD. My daughter, Lavern Meggett, remembers: "She'd be cooking breakfast every morning before school. We had to eat breakfast every morning. She'd say, 'A child can't learn on an empty stomach.'"

Just like with pancakes, lots of people see waffles as one of the most important breakfast foods. It's one I made in my house all the time. My children loved my waffles. They'd run in the kitchen before school and bring their plates to me, waiting in excitement for that first warm bite. These waffles cook until they get a nice crisp on the edges, while the center of the waffle maintains a light, fluffy texture, and preserves a nutty crunch from the chopped pecans. Serve waffles with just a bit of butter and syrup.

**1 large egg**

**⅓ cup (65 g) sugar**

**2 cups (250 g) self-rising flour**

**1⅓ cups (315 ml) milk, whole or 2%, plus more if needed**

**½ cup (105 g) Crisco shortening, melted**

**⅓ cup (75 ml) sour cream**

**⅓ cup (40 g) pecans, chopped**

Plug in your waffle iron, allowing it to get hot.

In a medium mixing bowl, use a wooden spoon to beat together the egg and sugar. Add the flour and 1 cup (240 ml) of the milk and gently stir the mixture until combined.

Add the melted Crisco. Stir gently until combined. The batter should stiffen a bit. Allow the mixture to sit and thicken for 3 to 5 minutes.

Fold in the sour cream and pecans. Add the remaining ⅓ cup (75 ml) milk and stir gently. If the mixture is too thick, add more milk, 1 tablespoon at a time, until it becomes a batter.

Spoon three heaping spoonfuls of waffle batter into the hot waffle iron. Cook until the waffle iron light goes on, or until golden brown. The edges should be slightly crispy. Cook the remaining waffles, and serve immediately,

# 6 | SWEETS, DRINKS & SAUCES

THERE SHOULD ALWAYS BE A BIT OF SWEETNESS IN A HOME. Baking bread, cakes, and pies brings a lot of joy to my house. A cold sugary tea can relax your worries. A boozy icing can make a cake disappear within an hour (I suggest grabbing your piece first!). Toast spread with pepper jelly can brighten up a cold morning. And a cold, icy treat for all of the neighborhood kids on a hot South Carolinian summer day? Those are the memories you just don't forget.

This chapter contains the many desserts, drinks, and sauces that have brightened up my life. It includes recipes I've cooked for years, and recipes from my children and grandchildren, like the sweet and crumbly Gullah Geechee chewies (page 253) recipe that came from my granddaughter Denise. Some of these desserts work best with the freshest produce you can find, but some dishes, like my banana bread (page 244), come out best with bananas that are a little too ripe. My drinks are made in big batches, so you can save them for a warm day, or make them for a large picnic. This chapter includes desserts that span seasons, so you've got the perfect sweet potato pie for Thanksgiving and a bright, fruity strawberry shortcake for the spring. These recipes bring me so much joy, and I hope they do the same for you.

# Apple Brown Betty

SERVES: 6 TO 8

THIS WAS ONE OF MANY DESSERTS I LEARNED HOW TO MAKE AT THE DODGE HOUSE. Layers of sugary crunch are in each and every bite, and the sweet and woody cinnamon flavor shines throughout the dish. The flavors of this dish represent fall and winter to me, so I bake this dish when I want a little spoon of comfort during the cooler months. Serve this dish with vanilla ice cream or whipped cream for a real treat.

**6 slices white or whole-wheat bread**

**7 apples (2½ pounds/1.2 kg), preferably Granny Smith**

**1 tablespoon ground cinnamon**

**¾ cup (110 g) raisins**

**¼ cup (½ stick/55 g) unsalted butter, cut into pieces**

**½ to ⅓ cup (110 to 145 g) packed brown sugar, plus more to taste**

**1 tablespoon cornstarch**

**¼ cup (60 ml) fresh orange juice (from 1 orange)**

Preheat your oven's broiler to 500°F (260°C), or its highest setting. On your oven's highest rack, broil the bread on both sides, about 7 minutes total. Remove the bread from the oven and let it dry out until crunchy.

Cut the bread into squares, and place one half of the bread squares in the bottom of a greased 9 by 13-inch (23 by 33 cm) baking dish.

Set the oven temperature to 350°F (170°C).

Wash, peel, core, and slice the apples.

In a large mixing bowl, combine the cinnamon, raisins, butter, brown sugar, and cornstarch. Add the apple slices and toss to coat. Spread half of the apple mixture over the bread in the baking dish and repeat the layering until the dish is full. Sprinkle the orange juice over the entire dish. Cover with foil and bake for 25 to 30 minutes, until the apples are cooked. Remove the foil and bake, uncovered, for 10 minutes until brown.

# Pie Crust

MAKES: 2 CRUSTS

THIS PIE CRUST WORKS FOR ANY OF MY PIES. Most of my pies require one layer of crust for the bottom and one for the top, but like I say, you cook to your taste. When making a pie crust, you always want to use all-purpose flour for the dough, because self-rising flour will make the dough too thick. Give this recipe a couple of tries, and you'll be surprised at how quickly you become a pie crust expert.

**1½ cups (190 g) all-purpose flour, plus about ½ cup (65 g) for the countertop**

**1½ teaspoons salt**

**3 heaping tablespoons Crisco shortening**

**7 tablespoons (105 ml) ice-cold water, plus more if needed**

In a mixing bowl, combine the 1½ cups (190 g) flour and the salt. With a knife, cut the Crisco into the flour until it is a little lumpy.

Add the cold water by the tablespoon, and mix together until the dough holds together. If needed, add more water by the teaspoon. Careful—the dough should not be too wet or get stuck to your hands. Do not overwork the dough, or it will become stiff.

Sprinkle ½ cup (65 g) flour on the countertop. Take the dough and work it on the floured area. Separate the dough into two balls.

Roll out the dough with a rolling pin as thin as possible, making two pie crusts. Place one in the bottom of a pie dish. You may use a small knife to remove or trim any extra crust. Use other for the top crust.

To prebake a single crust: Preheat the oven to 350°F (170°C). Bake the crust in the pie dish until golden, about 15 minutes, checking after 10 minutes: If the crust bubbles up during baking, pierce the bubbles with a fork and return to the oven to finish baking. Let cool completely on a wire rack. If you're making my chocolate cream pie (page 234), lemon meringue pie (page 237), or sweet potato pie (page 241), you may use a fork to press into the rim edges of the pie dish, securing the pie crust to the dish.

# Apple Pie

SERVES: 8

A GOOD APPLE PIE EVERY NOW AND THEN IS GOOD FOR THE SOUL. You'll want to use firm apples that won't turn to mush when baked.

**5 large apples of choice (about 2⅓ pounds/1075 g)**

**1½ cups (330 g) packed brown sugar**

**Juice from ½ lemon**

**¼ cup (½ stick/55 g) unsalted butter, cut into pieces**

**1 tablespoon cornstarch**

**1½ teaspoons ground cinnamon**

**Pinch of salt**

**Unbaked pie crust dough (page 231), one half of the dough used to line a 9-inch (23 cm) pie dish, one half rolled out for the top crust**

Preheat the oven to 350°F (170°C).

Wash, peel, core, and slice the apples.

In a large mixing bowl, mix together the brown sugar, lemon juice, butter, cornstarch, cinnamon, and salt. Add the apples, stirring until the apples are coated. Transfer to the unbaked pie crust. Cover the top with pie crust and pinch the pie crusts together around the rim to seal. With a fork or toothpick, punch a few holes in the top pie crust, so the pie can breathe. Bake for 40 to 45 minutes, until golden brown.

# Baked Apples

SERVES: 6

MY CHILDREN WENT CRAZY FOR BAKED APPLES. The coating of cinnamon-sugar can turn fresh or overly ripe apples into a winter treat. Red or green, these apples are lined up in a sweet, buttery glaze.

**6 apples of choice, cored and peeled**

**½ cup (100 g) sugar**

**1 teaspoon ground cinnamon**

**¼ cup (½ stick/55 g) unsalted butter**

**Raisins, to taste**

Preheat the oven to 350°F (170°C).

Slice each apple, horizontally, into three pieces, making apple rings. Place the apple rings in a large mixing bowl.

In a separate, small bowl, mix together the sugar and cinnamon. Add the cinnamon-sugar to the apple rings and toss to coat.

Arrange the apples in an ungreased 9 by 13-inch (23 by 33 cm) baking dish. Place a dot of butter and 2 or 3 raisins in the hole of each apple ring.

Add ¼ cup (60 ml) water to the dish. Bake for 25 to 30 minutes, until the apples are soft.

# Chocolate Cream Pie

SERVES: 8 TO 10

THE CHOCOLATE LOVERS IN YOUR LIFE WILL ADORE THIS PIE. This light filling benefits from a night in the fridge, which will allow the filling to fully firm up. The whipped cream topping adds another layer of sweetness, and helps to balance some of the chocolaty taste.

**3 ounces (85 g) Baker's unsweetened chocolate**

**1 cup (200 g) plus 2 tablespoons sugar**

**¼ cup (30 g) all-purpose flour**

**½ teaspoon salt**

**2½ cups (600 ml) milk, whole or 2%**

**4 large egg yolks, lightly beaten**

**2 tablespoons unsalted butter**

**1 teaspoon vanilla extract**

**1 baked (9-inch/23 cm) pie crust (page 231)**

**Sweetened whipped cream (page 242)**

Melt the chocolate in the top of a double boiler over simmering water.

In a mixing bowl, whisk 1 cup (200 g) of the sugar, the flour, and salt together with ½ cup (120 ml) of the milk until smooth. Add the egg yolks and the remaining 2 cups (480 ml) milk. Add this mixture to the melted chocolate, whisking well.

Stir constantly and cook over medium heat until thick and smooth, about 10 minutes. Add the butter and vanilla, stir until melted, then pour into the pie shell.

Let cool, then cover loosely and refrigerate the pie overnight to chill.

Spread the whipped cream over the chocolate.

# Peach Pie

SERVES: 10

PEACHES ARE THE STATE FRUIT OF SOUTH CAROLINA, SO WE TAKE GOOD CARE TO MAKE SURE OUR PEACH-BASED DESSERTS ARE DONE JUST RIGHT. This double-crust pie is a peach-filled culinary delight in every single layer. From the flaky, rich bottom pie crust, to the juicy, citrusy sweet peach filling, to golden browned crust on top, a peach pie is the type of dessert you bring to picnics, cookouts, and other summertime outings so you can share this good cookin' with the whole neighborhood. I prefer using lemon juice with the peaches because it enhances the flavor of the peaches. Vanilla extract would just smother the peach flavor.

**6 peaches (about 2 pounds/880 g), peeled, pitted, and sliced**

**¾ cup (150 g) granulated or ¾ cup (165 g) packed light brown sugar**

**¼ cup (½ stick/55 g) unsalted butter, cut into pieces**

**1 tablespoon all-purpose flour**

**Juice from ½ lemon**

**Unbaked pie crust dough (page 231), one half of the dough used to line a 9-inch (23 cm) pie dish, one half rolled out for the top crust**

Preheat the oven to 350°F (170°C).

Put the peaches in a mixing bowl with the sugar, butter, flour, and lemon juice. Stir until the peaches are covered.

Transfer to the unbaked pie crust. Cover the top with pie crust and pinch the pie crusts together around the rim to seal. With a fork or toothpick, punch a few holes in the top pie crust. Bake for 40 to 45 minutes, until golden brown and bubbling.

# Lemon Meringue Pie

SERVES: 8 TO 10

PEOPLE LIKE TO THINK OF LEMONS AS SUMMERTIME FRUIT, BUT THEY DON'T REALIZE THAT SOME OF THE BEST LEMONS ARE READY TO PICK DURING THE WINTER. That's when I like to make my lemon meringue pie. The filling for this pie will go to the top of the pie dish—this will not be a stingy pie.

**1 unbaked (9-inch/23 cm) bottom pie crust (page 231)**

FOR THE FILLING:

**½ cup (1 stick/115 g) unsalted butter, at room temperature**

**1⅓ cups (265 g) sugar**

**¼ cup (30 g) all-purpose or self-rising flour**

**7 tablespoons (55 g) cornstarch**

**Pinch of salt**

**4 large egg yolks**

**Grated zest from 2 lemons**

**¼ cup (60 ml) fresh lemon juice (from 2 lemons)**

FOR THE MERINGUE:

**4 large egg whites**

**¼ teaspoon cream of tartar**

**½ cup (100 g) sugar**

**½ teaspoon vanilla extract**

Preheat the oven to 350°F (170°C).

Bake the pie crust for 15 minutes. Set aside. Reduce the oven temperature to 250°F (120°C).

Make the filling: In a large mixing bowl, mix the butter, sugar, flour, cornstarch, 1½ cups (360 ml) water, salt, and egg yolks. Transfer to a steel bowl above a large pot of simmering water, or a double boiler on the stove. Cook over medium-high heat, stirring constantly, until the mixture thickens, 12 to 15 minutes. If the mixture becomes too thick and doesn't easily drip from a spoon, remove from the double boiler, beat with an electric mixer until smooth, and then continue.

Remove mixture from the heat and let cool.

After the mixture is cooled, add the lemon zest and juice and stir. Pour the lemon mixture into the par-baked pie shell.

Make the meringue: In a completely clean and dry mixing bowl, beat the egg whites with an electric mixer until smooth, about 4 minutes. Add the cream of tartar.

Beat until the mixture is foamy and almost forms peaks, at least 5 minutes. Slowly add the sugar, continuing to beat until fluffy. Add the vanilla and mix well. If the egg whites are beaten properly, the meringue will be smooth like sour cream. If the egg whites are beaten too long, the meringue consistency will be more like cottage cheese.

Spread the meringue over the lemon filling with a spatula.

Bake for 20 to 25 minutes, until cooked all the way through and the top is golden brown.

# Pecan Pie

SERVES: 8 TO 10

WHETHER IT'S FOR THANKSGIVING OR A DESSERT TO HAVE AROUND THE HOUSE, IT'S IMPORTANT TO KNOW HOW TO MAKE A GOOD PECAN PIE. With a layer of pecans on the bottom, this rich, nutty pie is an essential dessert during the Meggett family holidays. It's very important to let the pie sit for two hours before serving so the filling can settle, ensuring crisp, smooth slices.

**1½ cups (180 g) pecans, chopped**

**1 unbaked (9-inch/23 cm) pie crust (page 231)**

**3 large eggs**

**1 cup (240 ml) dark Karo corn syrup**

**2 tablespoons unsalted butter, melted**

**1 cup (220 g) packed brown sugar**

**1½ tablespoons all-purpose flour**

**1 teaspoon vanilla extract**

**Pinch of salt**

Preheat the oven to 350°F (170°C).

Spread the pecan pieces over the unbaked pie crust, covering the bottom of the shell completely.

In a mixing bowl, using an electric mixer, beat together the eggs, syrup, melted butter, brown sugar, flour, vanilla, and salt until combined. Pour the mixture over the pecans.

Bake for about 40 minutes, until just set in the center. Remove from the oven and allow the pie to cool for at least 2 hours before serving.

# Sweet Potato Pie

SERVES: 8 TO 10

IN OUR CULTURE, WE HAVE A RUNNING JOKE DURING THE HOLIDAY SEASON THAT USUALLY BEGINS WITH: "WHO BROUGHT THE SWEET POTATO PIE?" Nobody wants to eat a pie that's too crumbly, too soggy, too dry, or has too much going on. I've been making this pie for years, so when the family knows that I brought it to the table, all worries are thrown aside.

Making good sweet potato pie starts with picking good sweet potatoes. Small and medium sweet potatoes usually tend to be sweeter and creamier, which is exactly what you want for a holiday dessert. Don't be stingy with the sweet potato filling. You can cut the pie slice as narrow as you want, but you need to have plenty of sweet potato filling to make this dish that masterpiece it should be.

**7 small sweet potatoes (about 1¾ pounds/790 g), unpeeled**

**½ cup (1 stick/115 g) unsalted butter, softened**

**1 cup (220 g) packed brown sugar**

**¼ cup (125 g) all-purpose flour**

**2 teaspoons ground cinnamon**

**2 large eggs, beaten**

**1½ teaspoons lemon extract**

**1 unbaked (9-inch/23 cm) bottom pie crust (page 231)**

**Sweetened whipped cream (page 242)**

Preheat the oven to 350°F (170°C).

Wash and boil the sweet potatoes in 2 to 3 quarts (2 to 2.8 L) water until tender. Do not peel. Drain and allow the sweet potatoes to cool for 5 to 10 minutes.

Once cooled, remove the skins from the sweet potatoes. Place the flesh in a large mixing bowl. Beat with an electric mixer until all the "strings" are removed. Do this by mixing, stopping, removing the strings from the beaters, rinsing the beaters, and mixing again. Repeat this process four to six times until all the strings are gone.

Add the butter, brown sugar, flour, cinnamon, eggs, and lemon extract to the potatoes and mix all the ingredients together well.

Pour into the unbaked pie crust, filling to the top. Bake for 1 hour. Let the pie cool before serving. Slice and serve with whipped cream.

**VARIATION: For an even sweeter dish, instead of whipped cream as a topping, you can make a marshmallow topping for the sweet potato pie. Remove the sweet potato pie from oven after baking for 50 minutes. Sprinkle the top of the pie with single layer of mini marshmallows, and bake for the last 10 minutes of baking time, or until golden brown.**

# Sweetened Whipped Cream

MAKES: ENOUGH FOR 1 PIE OR CAKE

WHIPPING CREAM AND SUGAR IS ALL IT TAKES TO MAKE THIS VERSATILE TOPPING. It can also be used for strawberry shortcake or apple pie.

**1 pint (480 ml) whipping cream**

**2 tablespoons sugar**

In a medium-sized mixing bowl, with an electric mixer on high speed, beat the cream until peaks begin to form. While mixing, add the sugar. Continue to mix until stiff peaks form, 3 to 4 minutes total. Add a spoonful of this topping to each piece of pie before serving.

# Baked Bananas

SERVES: 5

BAKED BANANAS ARE A GOOD WAY TO MAKE USE OF TOO MANY BANANAS, OR BANANAS THAT ARE A BIT PAST THEIR PRIME. Once baked, add a little whipped cream and honey on top of each banana.

**5 bananas**

**1½ teaspoons ground cinnamon**

**¼ cup (55 g) packed brown sugar**

**1 teaspoon cornstarch**

**1 tablespoon honey, plus more for serving (optional)**

**Sweetened whipped cream (opposite), for serving**

Preheat the oven to 350°F (170°C).

Peel the bananas and place the whole bananas in a casserole dish. Sprinkle the bananas with the cinnamon and brown sugar.

In a separate bowl, combine the cornstarch and ¼ cup (60 ml) water, and pour the mixture over the bananas. Top the bananas with the honey, if desired.

Bake for 20 minutes, then serve topped with whipped cream and more honey.

# Banana Bread

MAKES: 2 LOAVES

BANANA BREAD IS ANOTHER GOOD WAY TO USE BANANAS THAT ARE VERY RIPE, OR A LITTLE BIT PAST THEIR PRIME. Because I learned to cook and bake for large groups, I still bake enough banana bread for two loaves. People love it so much, though, that sometimes two loaves isn't even enough!

**1 cup (2 sticks/225 g) unsalted butter, at room temperature**

**4 large eggs**

**2 cups (400 g) sugar**

**1 tablespoon vanilla extract**

**½ teaspoon almond extract**

**3 cups (375 g) self-rising flour**

**3 very ripe bananas, mashed (2½ cups/600 g)**

**½ cup (60 g) black walnuts or pecans, chopped**

Preheat the oven to 350°F (170°C). Grease and flour two 5 by 9-inch (12.5 by 23 cm) loaf pans, or one 10-inch (25 cm) Bundt pan.

In a large mixing bowl, beat together the butter, eggs, and sugar with an electric mixer. Add the vanilla and almond extracts and the flour.

Add the bananas and beat well. Stir in the walnuts. Divide the batter between the prepared pans.

Bake for 45 minutes to 1 hour. To test the bread for doneness, touch the top of the bread lightly. If the bread "springs back," or bounces a bit, it is ready. A skewer inserted in the center should also come out clean. Let cool for 5 minutes, then loosen the edges and turn out onto a wire rack to cool.

# Bread Pudding

SERVES: 8 TO 10

A DESSERT THAT MAKES GOOD USE OF LEFTOVERS IS MY KIND OF DESSERT. The best bread pudding uses stale or day-old bread. This is because when bread becomes stale, it becomes stiff and dry, and dry bread can absorb more liquid than fresh bread. In addition to milk, I also add pineapple juice as a liquid component. On Sundays, lemon pie, apple pie . . . it was all there. But this was the dessert everyone wanted after church. As soon as the bread pudding comes out of the oven, spread generous layers of my hard sauce on top, and enjoy watching it melt between the creases of the bread. You talk about a divine dessert? That's this pudding.

FOR THE BREAD PUDDING:

**5 large eggs**

**1½ cups (330 g) packed light brown sugar (granulated can be used, but brown is preferable for color)**

**1 cup (2 sticks/225 g) unsalted butter**

**1 cup (145 g) raisins**

**1 (8-ounce/227 g) can crushed pineapple, drained**

**2 teaspoons ground cinnamon**

**1 tablespoon lemon extract**

**1½ to 2 loaves day-old bread, pinched into pieces, but not flattened**

**4 cups (960 ml) milk, whole or 2%**

FOR THE HARD SAUCE:

**½ cup (1 stick/115 g) unsalted butter, at room temperature**

**¾ cup (165 g) packed light brown sugar**

**2 to 3 capfuls of rum, depending on taste**

Make the bread pudding: Preheat the oven to 350°F (170°C). Grease a 9 by 13-inch (23 by 33 cm) baking pan, or two 4 by 8-inch (10 by 20 cm) loaf pans.

In a large mixing bowl, use a wooden spoon to combine the eggs, brown sugar, and butter. Add the raisins, pineapple, cinnamon, and lemon extract to the egg mixture and mix again.

Add the bread pieces and the milk. Do not beat the mixture; simply fold it. The mixture should not be dry, but not too soupy.

Pour the mixture into the prepared baking pan or loaf pans. Bake for 1 hour, until golden brown. The bread should have soaked up the milk. There should be pieces of crust showing on the top of the bread pudding.

Make the hard sauce: In a large mixing bowl, using an electric mixer, beat the butter with the brown sugar until creamy. Add rum according to taste.

Pour the hard sauce over the warm bread pudding. Serve immediately.

**TIP: If I had any leftover rice, it wouldn't go to waste: I used to eat all the rum sauce on crackers!**

# Benne Cookies

MAKES: ABOUT 40 COOKIES

WHEN I WAS GROWING UP, I HAD NO IDEA HOW MUCH HISTORY WAS IN BENNE COOKIES. Also known as "benne wafers," benne cookies were just another sweet treat that we island folks loved to eat. In fact, I learned how to make these cookies at the Dodge House. A lady named Mamie Frances was the real pro, and she taught me how to make them just right.

As an adult, I found out that the benne seeds used for the cookie actually arrived to the United States with our African ancestors. Native to the African continent, benne seeds are often confused with sesame seeds. However, benne seeds have a much more distinct taste. They're nuttier, a bit smoky, and when toasted, they produce an intense, almost woody smell throughout the kitchen. Benne seeds have a rich history in the Sea Islands. Enslaved people cultivated these seeds in their own gardens, and eventually white slave owners took advantage of their crop and started use benne seeds to produce cooking oil. Their road in the United States has been long and complex, but thanks to the preservationist nature of Gullah Geechee people, they still grow across the Carolinas and Sea Islands today.

My benne cookies come from Mama, and she learned how to make them from generations before her. Thin and crisp, these cookies should be like wafers; you don't want them to rise.

**1 tablespoon margarine or butter, or more as needed (butter can be used to toast the benne seeds, but it burns more easily than margarine)**

**1 cup (140 g) benne seeds or sesame seeds**

**1 cup (125 g) sifted all-purpose flour**

**½ teaspoon baking soda**

**½ teaspoon salt**

**½ cup (1 stick/115 g) unsalted butter, at room temperature**

**½ cup (100 g) granulated sugar**

**¼ cup (55 g) packed light brown sugar**

**1 large egg, beaten**

**1 teaspoon vanilla extract**

Preheat the oven to 350°F (170°C). Grease two cookie sheets.

Melt 1 tablespoon margarine in a cast-iron skillet over medium heat and add the benne seeds, stirring to coat them—add more margarine if needed. Toast the seeds, stirring frequently, until fragrant and darkened a shade. Take care not to burn the seeds. Scrape onto a plate and let cool completely.

Sift the flour, baking soda, and salt together into a medium bowl.

In a large bowl, cream together the ½ cup (1 stick/115 g) butter and the sugars until well combined and fluffy. Add the egg and beat well. Add the cooled toasted benne seeds and the vanilla. Stir in the flour mixture.

Drop rounded teaspoonfuls of the cookie dough at least 2½ inches (6 cm) apart on one prepared cookie sheet. Bake for 8 to 10 minutes maximum, until golden brown around the edges. Remove the wafers from the cookie sheet immediately and place on waxed paper to cool. Repeat with the remaining dough on the second cookie sheet, reusing the first sheet when it's cooled.

# Cocktail Pecans

MAKES: 1 LARGE BATCH

COCKTAIL PECANS MAKE A GREAT SNACK OR APPETIZER. This is one of the few recipes where I use margarine, because if butter is used the pecans will burn more easily. If you have any leftovers, or plan on serving them later, you'll need to refrigerate them or they'll become rancid. You may serve these hot or cold.

**2 pounds (910 g) pecan halves**

**1½ sticks (170 g) margarine**

**Salt, to taste**

Preheat the oven to 200°F (90°C).

Spread the pecan halves in the bottom of a 9 by 13-inch (23 by 33 cm) baking dish. Cut the margarine into pieces. Cover pecans with the margarine pieces. Bake for 2½ hours, stirring every 30 minutes, until crunchy. While baking, the pecans will absorb the margarine.

Remove the pecans from the oven and sprinkle with salt to taste. Stir to mix. Spread pecans out on a brown paper bag or paper towel to absorb excess margarine.

# Chewies

SERVES: 10 TO 12

NOT TO BE CONFUSED WITH BLONDIES, WHICH USUALLY DON'T HAVE PECANS, CHEWIES HAVE BEEN IN THE GULLAH GEECHEE COMMUNITY FOR GENERATIONS. I actually didn't make chewies too much growing up, but my grandchild Denice, or "Niecy," as we like to call her, really enjoyed them and learned how to make them on her own. Her recipe requires a little bit of elbow grease when it's time to cut and serve, but the sweet, sweet payoff is well worth the energy.

**¾ cup (1½ sticks/170 g) unsalted butter**

**3 cups (660 g) packed light or dark brown sugar**

**3 large eggs, beaten**

**1½ teaspoons vanilla extract**

**3 cups (360 g) pecans, chopped**

**3 cups (375 g) self-rising flour**

**¼ cup (30 g) confectioners' sugar**

Preheat the oven to 350°F (170°C). Grease a 9 by 13-inch (23 by 33 cm) baking dish; for thinner bars, use a 10½ by 15½-inch (26.5 by 39 cm) jelly-roll pan.

In a medium saucepan, melt the butter over medium heat. Stir in the brown sugar until smooth. Remove from the heat and let cool for a few minutes.

Stir the egg and vanilla into the brown sugar mixture. Stir in the pecans, followed by the flour. Spread the mixture evenly in the prepared baking dish.

Bake for about 25 minutes if using a jelly-roll pan, 40 minutes if using a baking pan, until golden brown around the edges and firm in the center; a skewer inserted in the center will come out a bit damp. Sprinkle the confectioners' sugar lightly over the top.

Let cool completely in the pan before cutting. For an easier cut, turn the chewies out onto a cutting board, and cut into squares.

# Cracklin' Rolls

MAKES: 16 ROLLS

MY DAUGHTER ELIZABETH, OR DEE DEE, HAS TAKEN ON DESSERTS IN OUR FAMILY. Following my lead, she's come up with her own desserts, including these sweet rolls. Cream cheese wrapped in tubes of sugar-crusted bread, and all anyone can do is eat one—or two—or five. Dee Dee serves them warm or cold, but I like them warm, when you get that melt-in-your-mouth experience.

**1 (1-pound/455 g) loaf white bread, thinly sliced and crusts removed**

**1 (8-ounce/225 g) package cream cheese, softened**

**¾ cup (75 g) confectioners' sugar**

**1 cup (200 g) granulated sugar**

**1½ teaspoons ground cinnamon**

**¾ cup (1½ sticks/170 g) unsalted butter, melted**

Preheat the oven to 350°F (170°C).

Flatten the bread slices with a rolling pin.

In a large mixing bowl, combine the cream cheese and confectioners' sugar. In a separate bowl, combine the cinnamon and granulated sugar and set aside.

Spread about 1 tablespoon of the cheese mixture on each slice of bread. Roll up the bread, jelly-roll style.

Dip the rolls in melted butter, then in the cinnamon-sugar. Place on an ungreased baking sheet. Bake for 20 minutes, or until golden brown. You may serve these warm or cold.

# Lemon Cake

SERVES: 8 TO 10

LEMON CAKE IS A SIMPLE, YET DEEPLY PLEASANT DESSERT. I love this cake, because the lemon extract turns the batter perfectly fragrant—it's a refreshing dessert during the summer months. This lemon cake is best with rum icing (page 257), but it can also be served plain. If you don't have time to make the cake, you can always use a yellow cake mix and add lemon extract to it, for taste.

**4 large eggs**

**1 cup (2 sticks/225 g) unsalted butter, at room temperature**

**2 cups (400 g) sugar**

**3½ cups (440 g) cake flour, preferably Swans Down**

**3½ teaspoons baking powder**

**1 teaspoon baking soda**

**1 teaspoon salt**

**2⅓ cups (555 ml) milk, whole or 2%**

**½ cup (120 ml) full-fat buttermilk**

**2 teaspoons lemon extract**

Preheat the oven to 350°F (170°C). Grease a 10-inch (25 cm) Bundt pan or 9-inch (23 cm) round cake pan.

In a large mixing bowl, beat together the eggs, butter, and sugar until fluffy.

Sift the flour three times with the baking powder, baking soda, and salt. Add the flour mixture to the egg mixture and stir to incorporate. Stir in the milk, buttermilk, and lemon extract.

Pour the batter into the prepared pan. Bake for 45 to 60 minutes, until done. You may test for doneness by inserting a toothpick into the cake. The toothpick should come out clean.

Ice with rum icing, if desired.

# Rum Icing

MAKES: ENOUGH ICING FOR ONE DESSERT

MY RUM ICING GOES GREAT WITH MY LEMON CAKE (PAGE 257), BUT YOU CAN ALSO USE IT FOR YOUR OWN CAKES AND DESSERTS. The cream cheese makes the icing's texture fluffy and light, and the rum adds an extra kick that'll sweep you off your feet (or, as I like to say, slap yo' grandmama!). The walnuts give this icing a great crunch.

**2 (8-ounce/225 g) packs cream cheese, at room temperature**

**2 cups (440 g) packed light brown sugar**

**2 tablespoons butter, softened**

**¼ cup (60 ml) light rum, preferably Bacardi Superior**

**1 cup (120 g) black walnuts or pecans, finely chopped**

In a large mixing bowl, combine the cream cheese, brown sugar, and butter. With an electric mixer, beat until smooth.

Once the consistency is creamy, add the rum and mix again, then stir in the walnuts. Spread the icing over my lemon cake, or a cake or other dessert of your choosing.

# Sour Cream Cake

SERVES: 8 TO 10

I LOVE SOUR CREAM CAKE, NOT ONLY BECAUSE IT'S THE ONLY CAKE IN THIS BOOK THAT DOESN'T REQUIRE MILK (MORE ON THAT LATER), BUT BECAUSE IT'S SUCH A RICH TREAT FOR THE TABLE. Now, you've got to use your sifter here, because you want to remove all the lumps before adding the sour cream. You want a smooth consistency, a batter that's not too thick. If you do find that your mixture is too thick or lumpy, add no more than 3 tablespoons whole milk to the mixture before pouring it into the cake pan. Okay, sometimes you do need some milk after all!

**3 cups (600 g) sugar**

**1 cup (2 sticks/225 g) unsalted butter, softened**

**6 large eggs**

**3 cups (390 g) cake flour, preferably Swans Down**

**¼ teaspoon baking soda**

**1 teaspoon salt**

**1 cup (225 g) sour cream**

Preheat the oven to 350° (170°C). Grease an angel food cake pan.

In a large bowl, with an electric mixer, beat together the sugar, butter, and eggs.

In a separate bowl, sift the flour, baking soda, and salt together. Stir into the egg mixture, then add the sour cream. Mix together.

Pour the batter into the prepared pan. Bake for 1 hour. If the cake gets too brown on top before it's finished baking, cover with foil for the remaining time. Allow the cake to cool before removing from the pan.

# Pineapple Upside-Down Cake

SERVES: 8 TO 10

I LEARNED HOW TO MAKE THIS DISH AT THE DODGE HOUSE, BUT I MADE IT MY OWN BY CREATING MY OWN BROWN SUGAR CRUST, THE REAL STAR OF THIS DESSERT. Pineapple upside-down cakes can be found throughout the American South, but my cake is one of the lightest and perfectly sweet versions in South Carolina. If time is short, you can use a yellow cake mix instead of the cake batter.

FOR THE CRUST:

**1 cup (220 g) packed brown sugar**

**¼ cup (½ stick/55 g) unsalted butter, melted**

**1 (20-ounce/567 g) can pineapple slices**

**½ (10-ounce/283 g) jar maraschino cherries, drained**

FOR THE CAKE BATTER:

**2 large eggs**

**¾ cup (1½ sticks/170 g) unsalted butter, softened**

**2 cups (400 g) granulated sugar**

**2½ cups (325 g) cake flour, preferably Swans Down**

**2½ teaspoons baking powder**

**1 teaspoon salt**

**1 cup (260 ml) milk, whole or 2%**

**1 teaspoon vanilla extract**

FOR SERVING (OPTIONAL):

**Sweetened whipped cream (page 242)**

Preheat the oven to 350°F (170°C).

Make the crust: In a medium mixing bowl, combine the brown sugar and butter. Using a spoon, press the mixture into the bottom of a 10-inch (25 cm) round cake pan, ensuring that the bottom is fully covered.

Open the pineapple can, and drain the pineapple juice from pineapples, saving the pineapple juice. Place the pineapple rings on the brown sugar mixture in an arrangement of your liking. Place a cherry in the center of each pineapple ring.

Make the cake batter: In a large mixing bowl, using an electric mixer, beat all the ingredients and ⅓ cup (75 ml) of the reserved pineapple juice together. Once combined, pour the mixture over the pineapple.

Bake the cake for 45 minutes, or until done—an inserted toothpick should be clean when removed.

Remove the cake from the oven and allow it to cool completely. Once cooled, turn the cake upside down onto a cake plate. You will get to see your pineapple and cherries on the top. Slice and serve with whipped cream, if you'd like.

# Sweet Potato Cake

SERVES: 8 TO 10

SWEET POTATOES ARE NATIVE TO THE AMERICAS, BUT MY GOSH, LOOK AT WHAT BLACK FOLKS HAVE BEEN ABLE TO DO WITH THEM! Baked sweet potatoes, sweet potato pie, and sweet potato casserole are mainstays in American cooking, all thanks to Black Americans. In this sweet potato cake, my daughter Dee Dee added her own twist to this root vegetable. So light, so sweet, and so moist, this cake is a new chapter in our family's cooking legacy.

**1 medium sweet potato, baked and peeled**

**1 box yellow cake mix, preferably Pillsbury**

**4 large eggs**

**1 cup (200 g) sugar**

**¾ cup (180 ml) vegetable or canola oil**

**1 teaspoon grated nutmeg**

**1 teaspoon ground cinnamon**

Preheat the oven to 350°F (170°C). Grease and flour a 10-inch (25 cm) Bundt pan or 9-inch (23 cm) round cake pan.

Mix the sweet potato with an electric mixer to remove the strings. Do this by mixing, stopping, removing the strings from the beaters, rinsing the beaters, and mixing again. Repeat this process four to six times, until all the strings are gone.

Add the cake mix and stir together until smooth. Add the remaining ingredients and mix well. Pour into the prepared pan. Bake for 45 minutes, or until done. You may test for doneness by inserting a toothpick in the cake. If it comes out clean, get ready to enjoy some good eatin'.

## *THE POTATO SLIP*

You plant sweet potatoes in March, and you harvest in May. And then you take the vine from the potato, and you plant that on the Fourth of July. And then you dig that in November, and you get your slip—you save the little ones. You bank the little ones in a separate bank. And you save that to plant next year, in March. And when you plant that one, that'll be your root potato. 'Cause, see, they call it the root potato and the slip potato. So when you get the potato that you plant, the vine that you plant on the Fourth of July? That will be your root potato for you to plant next year. And when you plant that root potato next year, and folks come Fourth of July to plant that slip, that'll be your vine for your slip potato for next year. I'll never forget that. We always had to go plant the potato, and when you get through planting the potato, then the potato will grow and the vine would come. And every Fourth of July, we had to go in the field and plant the slip potato. That was a traditional thing for Edisto.

# Strawberry Shortcake

SERVES: 8 TO 10

WHEN MY CHILDREN DID A GREAT JOB IN SCHOOL, OR I WANTED TO BRING SOME EXTRA JOY TO THE HOUSE, I MADE MY FAMOUS STRAWBERRY SHORTCAKE. Now, the key to strawberry shortcake is picking the right berries for your dessert. If you have a local farm, buy your strawberries there. They'll likely be plumper, juicier, and, most important, sweeter than anything you'd find in the grocery store. If you do get yours from the store, search for strawberries that are completely red, plump, and free of bruises or wrinkles.

The biscuits for strawberry shortcake can also be made what we like to call "Sally Long Ways." Rather than cutting out circles for the biscuits, after kneading the dough, make a log-like loaf, roughly 3 by 8 inches (7.5 by 20 cm). You can bake this loaf, then cut the biscuits into any shapes you want—rectangles, squares, truly anything. You can use this bread for the strawberry shortcake or use it as breakfast biscuits for the next morning.

FOR THE BISCUITS:

**1 cup (205 g) Crisco shortening**

**1 large egg**

**¼ cup (50 g) sugar**

**2½ cups (315 g) self-rising flour, plus more for dusting**

**1½ cups (355 ml) milk, whole or 2%**

FOR THE STRAWBERRY FILLING:

**1 quart (665 g) strawberries**

**¾ cup (150 g) sugar**

FOR THE WHIPPED CREAM TOPPING:

**1 cup (240 ml) heavy cream**

**2 tablespoons sugar**

Make the biscuits: Preheat the oven to 350°F (170°C).

Using a spoon, beat together the Crisco, egg, and sugar. Once combined, add the flour and milk. Do not beat; simply fold the ingredients together until the flour is absorbed.

Sprinkle the countertop with a small amount of flour. Knead the dough until it holds together. Do not over knead. Roll out the dough and cut into biscuit-size pieces.

Place on a baking sheet and bake for 25 to 30 minutes, until browned. Remove from the oven and let cool. When cooled, split the biscuits in half with a fork. Place the bottom half of each biscuit on a serving plate and set the biscuit tops aside.

Make the strawberry filling and whipped cream topping: Clean the strawberries and set 1 whole strawberry per serving aside. Cut the remaining strawberries in half and mash them with a fork in a bowl. Add the sugar and mix gently.

Using an electric mixer, beat the cream until firm peaks form. Add the sugar and beat well.

Spoon strawberry filling onto the bottom half of each biscuit. Add a small amount of whipped cream to each. Place the biscuit tops and repeat with more strawberry filling and whipped cream. Place a whole strawberry in the center of each biscuit and serve immediately.

# Peach Cobbler

SERVES: 6 TO 8

IF YOU GO TO A PICNIC IN THE SOUTH AND THERE'S NO PEACH COBBLER, SOMEONE'S GOT SOME EXPLAINING TO DO. There's just nothing like biting into a cobbler of peaches cooked within a buttery crust. This recipe gets you a delicious cobbler in a fairly quick amount of time.

**6 medium peaches (about 2 pounds/880 g) (if smaller, use 8 to 10, if larger, use 4 to 6)**

**½ cup (110 g) packed light brown sugar**

**1 teaspoon fresh lemon juice**

**2 large eggs**

**½ cup (100 g) granulated sugar**

**½ cup (1 stick/115 g) unsalted butter, softened**

**2 cups (300 g) self-rising flour**

**½ cup (120 ml) whole milk**

Preheat the oven to 350° (170°C). Grease a 9 by 13-inch (23 by 33 cm) baking dish.

Wash, peel, and slice all of the peaches. Sprinkle the peaches with the brown sugar and lemon juice, and set aside.

With an electric mixer, beat together the eggs, granulated sugar, and butter. Add the flour and milk and mix all of the ingredients together, creating a batter.

Pour the batter into the prepared baking dish. Spoon the peach mixture over the batter.

Bake until golden brown, about 45 minutes.

# Vanilla Custard

SERVES: 6 TO 8

VANILLA CUSTARD IS A TIMELESS DESSERT. I enjoyed eating it as a child, my children enjoyed eating it when they were growing up, and to this day, people still reminisce on the good ol' days of eating a nice cup of custard. This is a recipe I've used since I started cooking, and I still enjoy it today.

**1½ cups (360 ml) milk, whole or 2%**

**2 large eggs, beaten, plus 3 large egg yolks**

**2 tablespoons unsalted butter**

**¼ cup (50 g) sugar**

**Pinch of salt**

**1 teaspoon vanilla extract**

Preheat the oven to 350°F (170°C). Grease 6 to 8 individual oven-safe dishes.

Scald the milk in the top of a double boiler over simmering water: heat just until bubbles form around the edges. In a small bowl, beat the 2 whole eggs. Add the eggs, butter, and sugar to the milk in the double boiler. Stir with a wooden spoon. When mixed, add the egg yolks, salt, and vanilla. Mix the custard again.

Fill the prepared dishes with the custard. Place the dishes in a baking pan and add enough water to come halfway up the sides of the dishes.

Transfer the baking pan with the dishes to the oven and bake for 45 minutes. Chill in the refrigerator for at least 3 hours, or until cold and thickened, and serve cold.

# Lemonade

SERVES: 6

AN ICE-COLD CUP OF LEMONADE IS A SUMMERTIME RITUAL. Fill your cup with some ice, sit on your porch or balcony, and enjoy this drink in peace.

**3 lemons**

**2 quarts (2 L) cold water**

**1¾ cups (350 g) sugar**

Roll the lemons across the countertop until they are soft. Cut them in half, and squeeze the juice into a 2-quart (2 L) pitcher. Remove any seeds with a spoon.

Add the water and sugar to the pitcher. Stir vigorously until the sugar is dissolved. Chill for at least 4 hours, or overnight.

# Chilly Bear

SERVES: 12

*Z'Nyiah Holmes, Emily's great-granddaughter*

SOMETIMES CALLED "THRILLS," CHILLY BEAR IS THE ICY TREAT OF THE SUMMER HERE ON EDISTO ISLAND. As a mom, if I made thrills, I'd be the star of the community. I'd hear my kids, running, "Mommy, can I have a chilly bear?!" I loved it. Seeing their faces covered in red juice dripping down their little mouths reminded me of the joy we find as a community, no matter where we live, how much money we have, or who we are.

Nowadays, my children and even grandchildren make chilly bears. They're so popular that some folks on the island will even sell them for a quarter each.

**1½ cups Tropical Punch Kool-Aid powder, or another red flavor**

**1 cup (200 g) sugar**

**3 quarts (2.8 L) water**

In a large bowl, mix the Kool-Aid, sugar, and water together. Stir the mixture until the Kool-Aid mix and sugar dissolve. Pour into 10-ounce (300 ml) Styrofoam cups, to about 1 inch (2.5 cm) from the tops.

Place the cups in the freezer, and leave them until frozen, at least 4 hours. The top should be glossy once frozen.

TIP: To eat a chilly bear, lick the top of the frozen treat several times, then push up from the bottom and flip the chilly bear over and back into the cup for more flavor. You can lick it, or eat it with a spoon until it is all gone. If it melts, just drink the Kool-Aid.

# Sweet Tea

SERVES: AT LEAST 12

SWEET TEA USED TO BE A LUXURY. Now, it's a common drink throughout the American South, and a lot of folks see it as a necessary part of the American summer. Sweet tea works best when it's kept simple. I would make two to three gallons for my church and community, and everyone got to enjoy more than one serving. While you're making the tea, it may look strong, but don't worry. The lemon will cut that bitter taste down.

**7 quarts (5.7 L) water**

**6 large black tea bags**

**3 lemons**

**1½ cups (300 g) sugar, plus more to taste**

Get two large pots. Pour 3 quarts (2.8 L) of the water into the first pot. This is the hot water pot. Bring to a boil over high heat. Put the teabags in the pot. Let the tea simmer for 3 to 4 minutes. Remove from the heat and let stand for 5 to 10 minutes.

In a separate large pot, pour 4 quarts (3.8 L) cold water. This will be the cold-water pot. Cut the lemons up into small to medium chunks and place them in the cold-water pot.

To the cold-water pot, add the sugar. The sugar here is to taste—if you want it sweet, add at least 1½ cups (300 g) sugar.

Remove the tea bags from the hot water pot. Pour the tea into the cold water pot, and remove the lemons. Stir the tea and taste it. Add more sugar if desired.

TIP: If the lemons are left in the tea too long, they will turn the tea bitter and leave an oily film.

*"Every day ain't going to be sugar, honey, and iced tea."*

# Muscadine Wine

SERVES: AT LEAST 10

MUSCADINE WINE IS A HOLIDAY WINE. It's a sweeter beverage and goes great with the holiday season; it has a refreshing taste. It takes some time to make, but it's well worth the wait. This wine has regional value, too. True to its name, muscadine wine comes from the muscadine grape, one of just a few grapes indigenous to the southeastern and south-central regions of the U.S. It emerged in the sixteenth century in Florida, and we've made it our own on Edisto. These grapes come red or green, so you can make red or white wine. You can use mason jars to store the wine for holiday gifts.

**5 quarts (4.7 L) muscadine grapes**

**1 (5-pound/2.3 kg) bag sugar**

Wash the grapes and put them in a 5-gallon (19 L) water jug. Grapes should cover the bottom of the jug, and reach the first ring.

Fill the jug to the top ring with tepid water. Close the jug. In a few days the grapes will start floating to the top.

Let the grapes and water sit for 3 months. The grapes will burst open and eventually float to the top, and the wine will begin to change colors.

Strain the juice through a cloth pillowcase or cheesecloth draped inside a bucket into a strainer or a colander. Be sure to squeeze the grapes to get all of the juice out.

Pull the pillowcase or cheesecloth from the bucket, rinse the pillowcase or cheesecloth, and strain again. Stir in sugar and put the contents back in the jug. Let wine sit for another 3 to 4 weeks. The longer it sits, the stronger it gets.

Strain again and, if needed, add more sugar to taste.

Pour the wine into quart- or pint-sized jars. The wine will keep for about 6 months.

# Applesauce

SERVES: 4 TO 6

THIS HOMEMADE APPLESAUCE WORKS BEST WITH RED APPLES. If you prefer a chunkier applesauce, eliminate the blender step. This applesauce goes great with pork.

**4 medium red apples (15 ounces/430 g)**

**Ground cinnamon, to taste**

**⅓ cup (65 g) white sugar**

Wash, peel, core, and slice the apples.

In a saucepan, cook the apples in ⅓ cup (75 ml) water over medium heat until soft, about 15 minutes. Remove the apples from the juice and save the juice for drinking.

Pour the apples into a blender with the cinnamon and sugar and blend until smooth.



# Orange Currant Jelly

MAKES: ABOUT 1 CUP (240 ML)

ANOTHER GOOD RECIPE FROM MY TIME AT THE DODGE HOUSE, THIS CURRANT JELLY IS A GOOD SAUCE FOR DUCK, VENISON, OR ANY TYPE OF WILD GAME (SEE PAGES 139 TO 173).

**¾ cup (180 g) currant jelly**

**¼ cup (60 ml) fresh orange juice (from 1 orange)**

Mix the jelly and orange juice together.

# Cocktail (Horseradish) Sauce

MAKES: ABOUT 1 CUP (240 ML)

MY HORSERADISH SAUCE IS ANOTHER SAUCE THAT YOU CAN MAKE YOUR OWN. It's simple to make, and just requires one night of cooling. This cocktail sauce is great for beef, pork, and lamb dishes.

**1 cup (240 ml) ketchup**

**1 teaspoon Worcestershire sauce**

**1 teaspoon fresh lemon juice**

**¼ teaspoon sugar**

**2 tablespoons prepared horseradish**

In a small mixing bowl, mix all of the ingredients together with a spoon. Cover and chill overnight.

# Pink Sauce

MAKES: ABOUT 1½ CUPS (360ML)

THE SMOOTH TEXTURE AND SUBTLE TASTE MAKE THIS A FAVORITE ON EDISTO ISLAND. People come by all the time just to get a bit of my sauce, and my children would ask me at the table, "Mommy, can I have some more pink sauce, please?" It's with good reason. This sauce is very versatile and goes with just about everything, from fried shrimp (page 80) to fried green tomatoes (page 129). With just a few ingredients and a minute or two of mixing, you've got a sauce that works with most seafood and fried vegetables. Not to mention, it's pretty to look at, too.

**1 small onion, grated**

**1 teaspoon Worcestershire sauce**

**1 teaspoon sugar**

**½ cup (115 g) mayonnaise**

**⅓ cup (75 ml) ketchup**

**1 teaspoon fresh lemon juice**

In a large bowl, mix all of the ingredients together.

# Pepper Jelly

MAKES: 10 HALF-PINT MASON JARS

EVERYBODY ON EDISTO KNOWS ABOUT MISS EMILY'S PEPPER JELLY. I've been making jars of this spicy, tangy jelly since I can remember. We eat it on toast, we put it on crackers, and we would serve it at big dinners when I worked at homes on Edisto. Now, I make jars to just give away to friends, neighbors, family, and anybody else who stops by. I hope you do the same.

**2 cups (480 ml) white vinegar**

**7 cups (1.4 kg) sugar**

**2 cups (290 g) diced yellow, red, orange, and green bell peppers**

**3 pouches Certo liquid pectin**

**2½ tablespoons vinegar-based hot sauce, plus more to taste, preferably Texas Pete**

In a large, heavy-bottomed pot, combine the vinegar and sugar. Bring to a boil over high heat.

Reduce the heat and let the mixture simmer for about 4 minutes. Add the peppers to the pot and bring back to a boil. Cook over low heat for 5 to 7 minutes. Remove from the heat and let cool for 20 minutes.

Return the pot to the stove over low heat. Add the Certo to the pot and cook for 3 minutes. Add hot sauce to taste and stir until combined.

Put the mixture back on the burner for 3 to 4 minutes, until it comes to a boil, stirring with a wooden spoon until you feel the texture thicken. Simmer for 3 to 5 minutes.

Remove from the heat. While still hot, carefully ladle the mixture into *sterilized* half-pint canning jars, leaving 1 inch (2.5 cm) of space at the top. Put the lids on and gently shake the jars (be careful, they're hot!) so that the peppers separate. If you'd like to store the jelly at room temperature, process them in a boiling water bath for 5 minutes (or longer depending on your elevation), following the instructions on the National Center for Home Food Preservation website. Let the jars cool on a towel on the counter overnight. As they cool, gently shake every so often so the peppers are evenly distributed in the jelly. If not processing the jars, keep them refrigerated.

## CHURCH SONG

*Rock of Ages cleft for me,*
*Let me hide myself in Thee,*
*Nothing in my hand I bring.*
*Simply to Thy cross I cling.*
*Naked, come to Thee for dress,*
*Helpless, come to Thee for grace.*
*While I draw this fleeting breath,*
*And my eye-strings break in death*
*Thou must save and Thou alone.*

*This was my grandmother's song—she used to sing it in church and to us at home.*

# ACKNOWLEDGMENTS

IF IT WASN'T FOR MY FRIEND AND FELLOW EDISTONIAN BECKY SMITH INSPIRING ME TO DO THIS BOOK, I MAY NOT HAVE DONE IT. When I was with her, she would just say, "You should write this book—all this wisdom, recipes, and these stories you have in your head. It would really be something." This is my book, and I have to give her credit for inspiring me. She and I spent years writing down all these thoughts and recipes together, because I only had them in my head.

My grandmother used to say: "You can feel people, and you can read people." And I said, "Now how can you feel people, and how can you read them?" But with Becky, there was just that feeling. Our differences never touched our deep connection, because our friendship is rooted in love. When your spirit meets my spirit, and my spirit meets your spirit, we have a connection.

When I met Becky, I said to myself right then: "Now, this is a friend for life." I want to thank the entire Smith family for their time, talent, and support helping me put this book together. I especially want to thank Mado Smith for capturing some of the early photos for the project, Elliott A. Smith for helping to develop a draft manuscript, and Sean Money and Elizabeth Fay for contributing their photography skills. Their help with the first drafts of this work helped this book come together. I'm so humbled and grateful to God for placing this family in my life.

I would also like to thank Jonah Straus from Straus Literary, BJ Dennis, and my editor, Holly Dolce. I want to thank Diane Shaw and the entire Abrams team for seeing my vision for this book. I'm so thankful for everyone who helped make this book real, including photographer Clay Williams and chef and food stylist Luciana Lamboy, as well as Terence Harvey and Jonathan Cooper. I want to thank my children for their love and support. I especially want to thank my daughters Marvette and Lavern Meggett for all of the time, energy, and love they gave to making sure this book came to fruition, from start to finish. And finally, I thank all of you for inviting me into your homes through food.

***LEFT TO RIGHT, FROM TOP:** Emily Meggett and Chef BJ Dennis's child, Mekhi Bennie Dennis; Emily and King's Farm Market owner Rett King; Emily's great-granddaughter Khadijah Ravenel; Emily and Becky Smith; Emily blessing the marriage of family friends Elliott and McKenzie Eddy Smith; Marsh Hen Mill owners Greg and Betsy Johnsman with Emily; Emily with her grandchildren Deanna Jones and Michelle Jones-Hutchinson; Emily's great-great-granddaughter Rosalina Goodwin; Emily with friend Linda Murray*

Live in

# INDEX

Editor: Holly Dolce
Designer: Diane Shaw
Managing Editor: Lisa Silverman
Production Manager: Anet Sirna-Bruder

Library of Congress Control Number: 2021946837

ISBN: 978-1-4197-5878-2
eISBN: 978-1-64700-690-7



Published in 2022 by Abrams, an imprint of ABRAMS.


Printed and bound in the United States
10 9 8 7 6 5 4 3 2 1